Apache Essentials

Install, Configure, Maintain

Second Edition

Darren James Harkness

Apress®

Apache Essentials: Install, Configure, Maintain

Darren James Harkness
Port Coquitlam, BC, Canada

ISBN-13 (pbk): 978-1-4842-8323-3
https://doi.org/10.1007/978-1-4842-8324-0

ISBN-13 (electronic): 978-1-4842-8324-0

Managing Director, Apress Media LLC: Welmoed Spahr
Acquisitions Editor: Divya Modi
Development Editor: James Markham
Coordinating Editor: Divya Modi
Copyeditor: Kim Burton

Cover designed by eStudioCalamar

Cover image designed by Freepik (www.freepik.com)

Distributed to the book trade worldwide by Springer Science+Business Media New York, 1 New York Plaza, New York, NY 10004. Phone 1-800-SPRINGER, fax (201) 348-4505, e-mail orders-ny@springer-sbm.com, or visit www.springeronline.com. Apress Media, LLC is a California LLC and the sole member (owner) is Springer Science + Business Media Finance Inc (SSBM Finance Inc). SSBM Finance Inc is a **Delaware** corporation.

For information on translations, please e-mail booktranslations@springernature.com; for reprint, paperback, or audio rights, please e-mail bookpermissions@springernature.com.

Apress titles may be purchased in bulk for academic, corporate, or promotional use. eBook versions and licenses are also available for most titles. For more information, reference our Print and eBook Bulk Sales web page at http://www.apress.com/bulk-sales.

Any source code or other supplementary material referenced by the author in this book is available to readers on GitHub (https://github.com/Apress). For more detailed information, please visit http://www.apress.com/source-code.

Printed on acid-free paper

To my own essentials, Chance and Kirsten

Table of Contents

About the Author

Like most of the world, **Darren James Harkness** started his coding career with "Hello world!" on a computer he bought himself at the local office supply store. Originally registered as a computer science major, he quickly learned there might be a different way to participate in technology better suited to his skill set than hard coding. From that point on, Darren turned to writing about the Web and managing smart people who do the same. He has never looked back.

Darren lives in the lower mainland of British Columbia, where he still spends too much time online, much to the chagrin of his partner, son, cat, and scruffy dog.

About the Technical Reviewer

**Massimo Nardone** has more than 25 years of experience in security, web/mobile development, cloud, and IT architecture. His true IT passions are security and Android.

He has been programming and teaching how to program with Android, Perl, PHP, Java, VB, Python, C/C++, and MySQL for more than 20 years. He holds a Master of Science degree in Computing Science from the University of Salerno, Italy.

He has worked as a CISO, CSO, security executive, IoT executive, project manager, software engineer, research engineer, chief security architect, PCI/SCADA auditor, and senior lead IT security/cloud/SCADA architect for many years. His technical skills include security, Android, cloud, Java, MySQL, Drupal, Cobol, Perl, web, and mobile development, MongoDB, D3, Joomla, Couchbase, C/C++, WebGL, Python, Pro Rails, Django CMS, Jekyll, Scratch, and more.

He worked as visiting lecturer and supervisor for exercises at the Networking Laboratory of the Helsinki University of Technology (Aalto University). He holds four international patents (PKI, SIP, SAML, and Proxy). He is currently working for Cognizant as head of cybersecurity and CISO to help clients internally and externally in areas of information and cyber security, like strategy, planning, processes, policies, procedures, governance, awareness, and so forth. In June 2017, he became a permanent member of the ISACA Finland board.

Massimo has reviewed more than 45 IT books for different publishing companies and is the co-author of *Pro Spring Security: Securing Spring Framework 5* and *Boot 2– based Java Applications* (Apress, 2019), *Beginning EJB in Java EE 8* (Apress, 2018), *Pro JPA 2 in Java EE 8* (Apress, 2018), and *Pro Android Games* (Apress, 2015).

Acknowledgments

I'd like to thank everyone who made this book possible. And believe me, this book wouldn't have been possible without a few people.

First and foremost is my partner Kirsten, who has been my biggest source of inspiration and strength. Without her support over the past 20-plus years, I wouldn't be where I am today. She has also been extremely patient while I spend time ignoring our little family to come back to a book I first wrote nearly 20 years ago.

Thank you to everyone who has worked with me and taught me what I didn't know. You know who you are, and there are far too many of you to list.

I also want to express my appreciation to the editors at Apress, who made some excellent suggestions while writing this book.

Finally, I want to thank all the propellerheads—past and present—that have worked to make Apache and the Web, in general, the great place that it is. Keep up the good work!

Introduction

Welcome to the second edition of *Apache Essentials*. Two decades ago, I started playing around with Apache—one of the most widely used web servers on the Internet. I had my site hosted on a friend's server, and I wanted to know more about the software running my domain. At the same time, I'd just come off a web design job where I had relied on two programmers to maintain the company's website and was completely at their whim whenever I needed something fixed or changed. Even a simple restart of the web server was out of my control.

Tired of waiting on people to do things for me, I decided it was time to start learning about Apache. The problem was that Apache was a completely foreign land to me, complete with sea monsters and wizards. I quickly hit a wall; there was no guide to Apache that talked to me as a designer in terms I could easily understand.

There are plenty of books and websites that are full of information about Apache and its configuration; however, they are written with the system administrator or programmer in mind. Designers are smart people, but having to read through pages upon pages of tech-speak is enough to scare anyone off.

I'm really quite stubborn, however. I kept struggling through the tech-speak, harassed my friend Alan, who ran my domain for me, and even installed Apache on my own computer so that I could learn how to use it.

After a little while, I'd learned enough about Apache that it was doing what I needed: serve web pages. Sure, I was speaking solely through the use of three-letter acronyms and had an odd desire to stay in dark places, but I think it was worth it in the end. Running a web server under Apache isn't nearly as scary as it appears. The benefits of knowing how Apache works and setting up my own environment were huge for someone learning to be a better web developer.

Out of that learning came the first edition of *Apache Essentials* in 2004. I wanted to share the knowledge I'd gathered so that other non-technical people could benefit. I didn't want anyone else to go through the same trials I did while learning how to use Apache or have to wade through pages of bland, technical jargon. I wrote this book as a friendly guide for web designers wanting to know a bit more about the system behind their websites, with clear instructions on how to get Apache up and running with scripting language support, secure website setup, and virtual domains.

Since then, I've installed Apache countless times on Linux servers, MacBooks, virtual private servers (VPS), and even Raspberry Pis. I run my own servers now and act as a resource for my staff when questions about hosting come up.

The first edition of *Apache Essentials* has stayed remarkably relevant to installing and configuring an Apache web server, as Apache's configuration has stayed consistent with earlier versions. Though not much has changed with the Apache web server in the past 20 years, the landscape around it has significantly shifted: sites are far more complex and use scripting languages more commonly than the static HTML sites of the early 2000s; performance is a more significant concern for the majority of websites, as users are far less patient with site load times; and troubleshooting issues on your site has become a core skill for anyone working on the Web.

The trade of web design and development has also shifted in this time; boot camps that push front-end developers and user experience designers through a compressed learning period have become exceptionally common, training a new generation of developers to rely on frameworks that speed up development but distance them from learning about the core technologies of the Web, such as the Apache web server. Folks receive just enough technical knowledge to get through a job interview; they don't get an in-depth understanding of the tools and systems they rely on. As a senior developer, manager, and now director, I've seen how this lack of understanding has been limiting for new digital professionals and affected their career development.

This edition of *Apache Essentials* is written to help support early career digital professionals. It provides an overview of the technologies they use daily, hoping that a greater understanding of them will help them grow in their careers. I've reorganized the chapters to include more information about configuring Apache for two common development languages, PHP and Node.js, and included a new chapter to help developers use Apache as a troubleshooting tool for their code regardless of what frameworks you might be using.

Chapters at a Glance

Chapter 1 covers the installation of Apache on macOS, Linux, or Windows and how to configure it for sending basic HTML files to your browser. By the end of this chapter, you'll have a basic understanding of Apache that we can build in later chapters.

Chapter 2 takes this further, exploring Apache's configuration options by setting up a basic HTML website. This chapter introduces you to Apache's configuration options and directives and some common configurations, such as protecting a website behind a username and password.

Chapter 3 explores configuring Apache for multiple development environments, letting you set up virtual domain names with the `.local` prefix—like `http://apachebook.local/`. This lets you test things in a more realistic way that matches a live website without having to put your development code in a publicly accessible location.

Chapter 4 goes a little further, configuring Apache to support scripting languages such as PHP and Node.js. The vast majority of modern websites use one of these scripting languages, whether in the form of a custom framework or a content management system like WordPress, Drupal, or Craft CMS.

Chapter 5 explains how to secure Apache. You won't necessarily need to do this for your local development environments, but this is critical for production sites.

Chapter 6 discusses Apache's log files, which are an exceptionally useful tool for troubleshooting things that might be wrong with your website. This chapter goes into more detail about the structure of log files and how to read them.

In Chapter 7, I share some sample Apache configurations with you and a GitHub repository where you can find them. You can use these to quickly set up sites and address common configuration needs.

Finally, a full list of the HTTP error codes can be found in the appendix.

Source Code

All source code used in this book can be downloaded from `github.com/apress/apache-essentials-2e`.

## CHAPTER 1

Getting Started with Apache

In this chapter, you learn how to install Apache safely on macOS, Linux, and Windows and get it up and running in its default configuration.

At the end of this chapter, you'll be able to load up your browser and visit `http://localhost/` to see a running default installation of Apache. But before we dive headlong into the guts of Apache, let's do a little review to get everybody up to speed.

How Web Servers Work

It's probably a good idea to start the review by explaining how a web server works. It's somewhat like the librarian at your local reference desk, acting as a front end to a store of information. When a web browser requests a file, the web server will process the request, search for the location of the file requested, then respond with what it found. On the surface, it's pretty simple. Of course, there's a lot of action happening behind the scenes invisibly (see Figure 1-1).

© Darren James Harkness 2022
D. J. Harkness, *Apache Essentials*, https://doi.org/10.1007/978-1-4842-8324-0_1

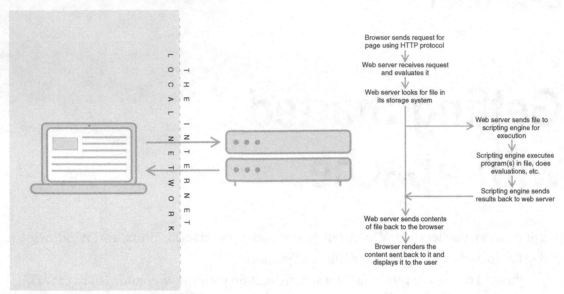

Figure 1-1. *A typical workflow for showing a web page*

The HyperText Transfer Protocol

A network is best thought of as a combination of communication layers; each layer represents a method of communication and is assigned a unique connection point known as a port number; there are 65,536 ports available in all, and many of those are reserved for known network protocols. One of these reserved ports is for HyperText Transfer Protocol (more commonly known as HTTP), which communicates on ports 80 and 443 (other examples of TCP ports include POP email (port 110) and FTP (which uses ports 20 and 21)).

The HTTP protocol is a common language for transferring hypertext data between a web server and a web browser. In short, it's how the client and server talk to each other. I'm not going to delve deeply into the protocol, but a sample HTTP transaction would look like the following.

```
GET /index.php HTTP/1.1
Host: www.apachebook.com
HTTP/1.1 200 OK
Content-Type: text/html; charset=utf-8
Content-Length: length
<DATA>
```

The transaction starts when the browser requests a file from the web server (GET `http://www.apachebook.com/index.php`). When this request is received, the web server checks to see if the file exists at the location specified and if the browser has permission to view the page. If an error is encountered, the web server will return the error to the browser, often followed by a brief explanation of the error. The most common of these errors is 404 (file not found), 403 (forbidden), or 500 (script error).

If everything is fine, the web server will return a 200 OK, then start streaming the file's content to the browser. Whenever an `<img>` tag (or any other tag that references additional files, such as the `<object>` or `<link>` tag) is encountered, the process repeats itself. In the end, the browser receives all the information on the web page and renders it according to the HTML sent. Since web pages often reference one or more graphic files, a full HTTP transaction could look as follows.

```
GET https://www.apachebook.com/index.php
200
<data>
GET https://www.apachebook.com/styles.css
200
<data>
GET https://apachebook.com/img/ae_logo.svg
200
<data>
```

A full list of the HTTP error codes can be found in the appendix.

A (Very) Brief History of Apache

In June of 1991, the first web server was born in the most ironic of locations. In a room at CERN (a particle physics laboratory in Geneva, Switzerland), the first version of httpd (HyperText Transfer Protocol Daemon) was created. Little did they know they would be opening the door to an entirely new universe. Or, maybe they did; it was a physics lab, after all.

Tim Berners-Lee, the creator of the Web, first started working on the basic concept of linked documents as early as 1980 while on a short contract with CERN. While there, he created Enquire, a program used privately to store information using random associations. Though never published, a seed was planted firmly in his mind. When he returned to CERN in 1989, he brought a massive improvement to Enquire.

The World Wide Web (WWW), as Berners-Lee called it, was Enquire on a global scale. The basic idea behind WWW was to allow a group of high-energy physicists to combine their knowledge into a library of interconnected work. Are you referring to a colleague's paper on quantum mechanics? Why merely cite the paper and leave it up to the reader to search through a library for it when you can just provide a link to it within your own paper?

In 1991, after a year or so of internal development at CERN, Berners-Lee released httpd (the first web server) and WorldWideWeb (the first web editor and incidentally the first WYSIWYG editor) to the public at large through the Internet and made their own HTTP server publicly accessible. The idea hit the 'net and exploded. According to Berners-Lee, the load on the CERN web server grew by a factor of 10 every year. Berners-Lee spent the next three years defining the language of the Web—HTML—and further developing the httpd web server, working heavily with feedback from the Web's early adopters.

Around the same time, the National Center for Supercomputing Applications (NCSA) was working on its own version of the httpd server. Complaining that the CERN web server was "too large and complex", Rob McCool (yes, his actual name) worked with several others at NCSA to create a leaner, simpler version of the web server. He worked on NCSA's web server until 1994, when—as Apache's timeline states—he "left to get a real job." (In fact, he left to help form Netscape, one of the first widely-used commercial web browsers).

When Rob McCool left the httpd project, development crept to a halt. By early 1995, as the Internet became more accessible to the general public, use of the Web started booming, and webmasters soon discovered that httpd could no longer serve their needs adequately. As a result, in February 1995, eight brave souls started working together to develop the next generation of web servers—Apache. Working from the source code for httpd, these developers started writing patches to the NCSA httpd server (and according to Apache's history, the name "a patchy server" was born). In April 1995, the group made the first official public release of the Apache web server.

Over 25 years later, it is a thriving open-source community project with hundreds of developers regularly contributing source. In 1999, the Apache Software Foundation (ASF) was created as an official entity to help organize developers and provide legal and financial support. Apache powers more than 286 million sites, and it serves 45% of the

Web's busiest sites.[1] It's available for any operating system that has networking, including Linux, Windows, macOS, and even long-lost systems like OS/2 and BeOS.

Before You Begin…

Like any grand adventure, there are some things you must prepare before you embark on your quest. You'll want to keep notes, become familiar with your operating system's terminal or command line, gather documentation, and do resource planning.

Keep Notes

Keep running notes in your favorite notes application or desk-side notebook. There will be several points throughout this book where you must refer to various directories and configuration options, and having quick access to these will be helpful.

Get Familiar with Your Terminal

Regardless of which operating system you choose to install Apache, you must be comfortable with the command line or terminal. This text-only interface to your computer unlocks the ability to access parts of your computer that are normally hidden behind your desktop UI. For macOS, Linux, and Windows (using the Linux subsystem), this is critical for accessing and editing the configuration files for Apache and other elements.

As you move through this book, several examples use the command line to access and modify configuration files. It's highly recommended that you become comfortable starting up a terminal and learning its basic commands.

On macOS, the command line is accessed through **Terminal**, which can be found in the **Applications ➤ Utilities** folder in Finder. You can also use Spotlight to find the Terminal application quickly.

On Windows, the command line is accessed through the **command prompt** (cmd. exe), which can be found in the **Windows System** folder in the Start Menu. You may also install **PowerShell** through the Windows Store, which provides some extra tools for navigating the command line.

---

[1]`https://trends.builtwith.com/websitelist/Apache/Very-High-Traffic-Volume`

On Linux, the command line is accessed directly (if no desktop GUI is installed) or through a terminal application. On Ubuntu, this can be found by clicking **Show Applications**, opening the **Utilities** folder, and clicking **Terminal**.

Several courses and resources are available to help you learn about the command line, such as tutorials by Ubuntu[2] or The Odin Project[3] for UNIX-based terminals and Microsoft's documentation for its command prompt and PowerShell.[4]

Be Prepared to Read Documentation

I will cover most of what you need to know to get Apache set up and running on your computer. That said, I cannot cover all possibilities, and you will likely run into situations that aren't described in this book. For that, make sure you've got the documentation at hand for Apache on your operating system.

- Apache: `https://httpd.apache.org/docs/current/`

- Homebrew: `https://docs.brew.sh`

- XAMPP: `www.apachefriends.org/docs/`

- Ubuntu: `https://help.ubuntu.com`

What to Know Before Installing Apache

There are a few things you need to consider before installing Apache. These include which operating system to use, what additional software is needed, and which version of Apache to install.

A useful exercise at this point is to write a quick requirements document. If you are moving an existing website from a hosted server to your own server, find out how busy your web server has been and what technologies were used for it. If you are just starting up or don't have access to your web server's statistics, you need to estimate your server requirements. In both cases, you should ask the following questions.

---

[2] `https://ubuntu.com/tutorials/command-line-for-beginners`

[3] `www.theodinproject.com/paths/foundations/courses/foundations/lessons/command-line-basics-web-development-101`

[4] `https://docs.microsoft.com/en-us/windows-server/administration/windows-commands/windows-commands`

How complex is your site? The more complex the site, the busier the web server. If you are experiencing heavy traffic, the web server slows down significantly. It also needs more RAM to keep the site in its working memory. The best way to mitigate this is by increasing the amount of RAM allocated to the server.

Which scripting environments are currently being used for the website? Apache supports most scripting environments (PHP, Node.js, etc.), and some run better under Apache. Apache can even be configured to indirectly support .NET (C#) sites, though it requires a more advanced setup than what's covered in this book.

How large is the website, and how long do I want to keep server logs? With the growth in services like Amazon S3 and advances in hard drives, storage drive space is cheaper than ever. Add as much hard drive space as you can afford to. Modern websites often have significant storage needs for uploaded assets, frameworks, and libraries. You also want to provide space for your website's logs. The longer you keep log data, the more information you have to work with when building website statistics or troubleshooting issues.

Who do I want to have access to the web server? This is probably the most important question to ask. Anyone who has access to the web server machine also has access to the website stored on it. Though you can secure the website's directories under both Linux and Windows, it's not 100% secure so long as a user has access to the drive. If you use tools like ngrok or port forwarding on your router to provide outside access to your web server, this is especially important. That said, you will most likely be setting this up on a personal laptop or desktop machine, using Windows or macOS. Going forward, this is referred to as your *development environment*.

Using the Right Development Environment

It's *never* a good idea to make changes to your live website. Your website is your organization's digital presence in the world; you only want to update it when you are completely certain your code is good and bug-free.

To create this stability, most developers use a tiered set of environments that become more as you move through them. These start with an unstable development environment and end with a stable, tested production environment. Generally, developers use four environments (see Table 1-1), though this can reach up to six environments when using continuous integration.

Table 1-1. *Deployment Environments*

Environment	Description
Local Development	This is a sandbox for the developer to test code on as they write it. This is often their desktop or laptop, though a dedicated computer on their network may also be used as a development environment (a Raspberry Pi, for example).
Testing	The environment where more formal testing is performed. A quality control team ensures that the new code does not impact the existing functionality and tests major functionalities of the system after deploying the new code in the test environment. It is most commonly a server located within a corporate network or on a dedicated server outside the network.
Staging	A mirror of the production environment used for user acceptance and validation. It is generally available over the Internet but hidden from search engines and may be behind some form of authentication.
Production/Live	This is your live website, available to anyone over the Internet.

Adapted from https://en.wikipedia.org/wiki/Deployment_environment

This book only concerns the first tier, where you will build and check your code. This is the local development environment and, most commonly, your own laptop or desktop. In the coming chapters, I'll show you how to install and configure Apache on this environment so that you can view and test your website code in real time, regardless of whether you're connected to the Internet.

Apache can be run on virtually any commercial operating system. If it can connect to a network, chances are there's a version of Apache available for it. This book focuses primarily on macOS since it's currently the most used operating system among digital professionals. I'll point out the differences between macOS, Linux, and Windows as they emerge.

Apache vs. Other Web Servers

Apache is just one of many different web server applications available in a development environment, including free applications such as Nginx and Node.js's built-in app server and licensed applications such as Microsoft's Internet Information System (IIS) and Litespeed. On the surface, they seem to operate similarly (after all, they provide the same basic functionality), but underneath, each web server application has its own benefits and quirks.

Although Apache is the most commonly used web server, it's still useful to compare it to the other available options.

Choosing Apache Over Nginx

Apache and Nginx (pronounced "engine x")[5] are the two most popular web servers as of this book and have a roughly equal share of the web server market for public websites. They are often used together to provide a robust web service for high-traffic websites. In fact, that's why Nginx was originally developed as a supporting tool for Apache that helped solve a performance problem.

In the early 2000s, the amount of website traffic had been growing to the point where Apache could not handle all the simultaneous incoming requests. It had a rough limit of 10,000 requests at the same time.

That seems like a lot of requests, right? However, you must consider this: modern websites often have dozens of associated files on any page: style sheets, JavaScript files, and images or other media. Add to that functionality that requires the page to make additional requests asynchronously, such as accessing an API, which adds up very quickly. If you consider an average of 70 requests per page on a website,[6] that

---

[5] www.nginx.com/about/the-nginx-name
[6] https://httparchive.org/reports/state-of-the-web#reqTotal

means only about 140 to 150 people can access a website at the same time without experiencing issues.

Nginx was developed as a front-end proxy for Apache that would quickly serve static files, such as HTML, CSS, JavaScript, and images, and pass more computationally-involved scripts (such as PHP) to Apache to process separately. The combination of the two removed the 10,000 connections limit in Apache alone and set the stage for a highly performant web.

There are some downsides to using Nginx, however. First, it's more complicated to configure than Apache, as it uses a scripting-like format for its configuration files. Nginx doesn't allow directory-level overrides (discussed later), which lets you test configuration on the fly without restarting the server. Finally, Nginx is less flexible for scripting languages such as PHP, as it needs to pass these to separate applications to be interpreted and run (often through Apache).

All these decisions are made for better performance for high-traffic web servers, where milliseconds add up quickly over a large number of connections. To set up a development environment, however, Apache on its own is more than sufficient. You won't ever have any concerns around server performance or high loads due to many concurrent site visitors on your development environment. You won't see any benefit from using Nginx.

If you're interested in learning more about Nginx, check out Rahul Soni's excellent *Nginx: From Beginner to Pro* (Apress, 2016).

Apache over npm start for Node Development

Node.js is *very* friendly for on-the-fly testing in your browser. It lets you quickly start up a node application on a custom port by running `node app.js` and accessing the port on localhost (e.g., `http://localhost:3000`). This is great for very quick testing.

The downside is that the site is only available so long as the node application you started runs in your terminal, and you don't mind accessing things through non-standard URLs. If you close the terminal window or quit the node program, your testing server dies with it. If you try to access `http://localhost/` without supplying the port, you will not be able to view your Node.js project.

Apache can be configured to work with Node.js, however, and create an always available Node.js server that's accessible without supplying a custom port number. This is covered in more detail in Chapter 3.

Obtaining Apache

Apache has a few system requirements, but they're not nearly as bad as you might think. The first of these is disk space. Apache needs a jaw-dropping 50 MB to install. After it's installed, it needs only 20 MB to run. No, that's not a typo. One of the strengths of Apache is its lean nature. Similarly, you don't need much RAM or a powerful processor either; Apache runs on as little as 0.5 GB of RAM on a 1 GHz CPU if running a UNIX-based system such as Linux. If you follow the system requirements for your operating system, you stand a good chance of being able to run Apache. For comparison, Microsoft's Internet Information Server (IIS) requires at least a 1.4 GHz CPU, 2 GB of RAM, and 32 GB to operate.[7]

I'd suggest giving your Apache web server as much RAM and hard disk space as possible, however, and spending a little less on the processor unless you plan on using your server heavily or accessing a database frequently. The more RAM you have available for Apache, the happier it is and the faster it performs. And keep in mind it is running alongside other applications, such as your code editor and browser, which all compete for access to RAM and disk space as well as any database servers or scripting environments you may be using, such as PHP or Node.js.

Installing Apache on macOS

As of macOS 12, Apache is already installed on macOS. However, it's configured very basically, disabled by default, and doesn't have some of the libraries needed to support scripting, such as the PHP module. Given the direction Apple has been taking to keep macOS focused on its most common users, it's entirely likely that Apache itself will be removed in the future. Beyond that, there are a series of other pros and cons highlighted in Table 1-2.

---

[7] https://docs.microsoft.com/en-us/windows-server/get-started/hardware-requirements

Table 1-2. *Advantages and Disadvantages of Using macOS*

Advantages	Disadvantages
You probably already use a Mac in web design, UX, or web development, as they're popular within those disciplines.	macOS has a built-in version of Apache that might interfere with the operation of the version installed in this chapter.
macOS, like Linux, is built on a UNIX core, which gives you a very stable and secure environment on which to develop.	Apple's shift to their own proprietary CPU in 2021 initially added some performance and compatibility issues.
Apple provides several other developer-friendly tools through XCode, like Git, SCP, and SSH.	Apple's computers are priced at a premium, making them more expensive than other commodity desktops or laptops.
With its roots in UNIX, macOS was born and raised as a multiuser operating system that could handle multiple users and run multiple applications.	

Installing Apache Through Homebrew

While you can enable and configure the built-in Apache as a development environment, I suggest that you use Homebrew. This tool provides the ability to install packages such as Apache, PHP, and many other UNIX tools.

I recommend that you use Homebrew,[8] a package manager for macOS that makes it a bit easier to install and manage software packages like Apache, PHP, and MySQL (among many others). Homebrew has been actively maintained for macOS as an open source project since 2009 by a team of dedicated contributors. It provides a safe way to install this kind of software on your system without interacting with the core operating system.

Brew installs tools locally, outside of the protected system directories in macOS. This also makes it simpler to modify configuration files since you don't have to use administrator privileges to do so.

To install Homebrew, visit `https://brew.sh` and follow their installation directions. I'll wait.

---

[8] `https://brew.sh`

Once Homebrew is installed, you can install the Apache web server. Open your terminal application, and type in the following.

```
brew install apache2
```

This starts the installation process and puts a local copy of the Apache httpd server into your computer's /usr/local/ directory.

The following is an example of what you see in your terminal window.

```
swiftly:httpd darren$ brew install apache2
Updating Homebrew...
==> Auto-updated Homebrew!
Updated 3 taps (homebrew/core, homebrew/cask and homebrew/services).
==> New Formulae
rizin                                   symengine
==> Updated Formulae
Updated 194 formulae.
==> Updated Casks
Updated 144 casks.
==> Downloading https://ghcr.io/v2/homebrew/core/httpd/manifests/2.4.51
Already downloaded: /Users/darren/Library/Caches/Homebrew/downloads/a272ee
deda41a82ae9ab973e0e620883a524607fb315d48915f9bc82a3e6a628--httpd-2.4.51.
bottle_manifest.json
==> Downloading https://ghcr.io/v2/homebrew/core/httpd/blobs/
sha256:a1f6272efc48
Already downloaded: /Users/darren/Library/Caches/Homebrew/downloads/5fa3d8
4c175b5d968c6bfad6763a753afbb4486fe4e3307a00c87b2f9cc3a689--httpd--2.4.51.
monterey.bottle.tar.gz
==> Pouring httpd--2.4.51.monterey.bottle.tar.gz
==> Caveats
DocumentRoot is /usr/local/var/www.
The default ports have been set in /usr/local/etc/httpd/httpd.conf to 80
and in /usr/local/etc/httpd/extra/httpd-ssl.conf to 443 so that httpd can
run without sudo.
To restart httpd after an upgrade:
  brew services restart httpd
```

```
Or, if you don't want/need a background service you can just run:
  /usr/local/opt/httpd/bin/httpd -D FOREGROUND
==> Summary
  /usr/local/Cellar/httpd/2.4.51: 1,660 files, 31.6MB
swiftly:httpd darren$
```

That's a lot of text! You can ignore most of that, but there are a few important things about Homebrew to pay attention to.

- It lists the DocumentRoot as /usr/local/var/www. DocumentRoot is an Apache configuration directive explored in more detail in the next chapter. For now, just know that this is the directory where the website's files live on your computer and are accessible to the browser. On install, this contains an empty cgi-bin directory and an index.html file.

- It lists the default ports Apache is configured for. In the preceding example, these are ports 80 and 443 (for secure web). Do note that if you have enabled the built-in copy of Apache in macOS, these ports may be different, such as 8080 and 80443.

- It provides you with the command to start up Apache manually: /usr/local/opt/httpd/bin/httpd -D FOREGROUND. It's better to set this up as a service, however, so you don't have to remember to start Apache up every time you reboot your computer.

Running Apache as a Service Through Homebrew

Apache can be run when you need it using the preceding command, or it can constantly run as a background service on macOS. Running a program like Apache as a service is a bit more convenient, as it starts every time you restart your computer.

You can use Homebrew's built-in service manager to keep it running as a service. Type the following into your terminal.

```
sudo brew services start httpd
```

Once you've done that, you can skip to the "Basic Configuration" section at the end of this chapter.

Installing Apache on Linux

Linux offers the security and stability of a UNIX system without the cost; the Linux operating system (as well as the bulk of applications available for it) is placed under the General Public License (GPL) and made available to all, free of charge. It's developed under the philosophy of open source and, as such, is generally rock solid and secure. There is also a large range of low-cost hardware available that is compatible with Linux, such as the Raspberry Pi or an old desktop system sitting in a closet.

Since Linux itself consists solely of the basic operating system (and no applications or utilities), it has been packaged with a set of applications and utilities and a method of installation by several organizations. These different packages are called distributions; if you choose to install Linux, the fastest and easiest way is to decide upon a distribution.

There are hundreds of distributions to choose from, but only a few are generally accepted by most Linux developers, including Ubuntu, Debian, and Red Hat. Ubuntu is the most commonly used for desktop or laptop installations, with Debian often used for server installations.

However, a problem with using Linux is that there is likely a larger initial learning curve if you aren't already familiar with it. Though Linux does have a graphical desktop, most administration is done through a text-only command-line interface. As a result, there's a new set of commands that you must learn and remember. However, most—if not all—of the information you might need about Linux is readily available on the web.

For quick reference, Table 1-3 lists the advantages and disadvantages of installing Apache on Linux.

Table 1-3. *Advantages and Disadvantages of Using Linux*

Advantages	Disadvantages
Linux is far more secure, stable, and reliable than Windows. Due to the open nature of development, vulnerabilities are found and repaired quickly by Linux developers. Patches are often available within hours of a vulnerability being reported.	Linux offers an unfamiliar interface; most administration is done through the command-line interface.
With its roots in UNIX, Linux was born and raised as a multiuser operating system that could handle multiple users and run multiple applications. The Linux development team has decades to hone this ability and make sure that it handles multiple users with far more ease than Windows.	No single commercial entity is responsible for Linux, which might go against some corporate IT policies. All major Linux kernel (the core operating system) releases go through a rigorous code-review process administered by a dedicated community of developers sponsored by the Linux Foundation.
Linux performs better than Microsoft Windows since very little processing power goes into the display.	Linux has a larger learning curve than macOS and Windows.
Linux is built for network performance. Every major Linux distribution comes with the network tools needed to get a web server up and running.	Graphical administration tools aren't available for all system functions. You're going to need to be comfortable with the command line.
Linux offers far better remote management capability. Several methods, including Secure Shell (SSH) and remote desktop, allow you to connect to your server quickly and efficiently.	No commercial support is available for some distributions.
Linux is much more modular than other operating systems. The operating system needs only a couple hundred megabytes of disk space, and you only install the applications you want to use on the server.	The configuration directory structure is different from what Apache recommends. This can cause confusion if you are looking at examples online.

(continued)

Table 1-3. (*continued*)

Advantages	Disadvantages
Linux servers rarely need to be rebooted; all system services and applications can be modified or reinstalled without a reboot.	
Linux has a much lower cost of entry than the other operating systems, which makes it easier and inexpensive to have a separate dedicated development server apart from your personal workstation. You can even install it on an entry-level Raspberry Pi for a fraction of the cost for Windows or Mac.	

Choosing the Source Installation

Apache is and always has been open source software. This means that the source code is available for anybody to download, read, modify, and recompile. The source code is a series of instructions and commands that define individual functions (for example, reading the contents of a file and placing it in memory). These functions, when bundled together, create a complete application. However, to get to the application from the source code, the application must be compiled for your operating system (translated from the programming language source code to an executable file and its supporting library files).

One of the strong benefits of using open source software is security. Apache's source code is reviewed by literally thousands of eyes and is developed by a group of programmers who volunteer their time.

What does that mean to you? It means two things: quality and security. Because Apache is developed in an open environment, the greater the likelihood that bugs, vulnerabilities, and security problems are found. Even if a bug slips through, it is generally found and corrected in a matter of days.

But that doesn't tell you why you should choose the source install, does it? The source install is used for one of three purposes.

- **Customizing the application**. Some people installing the Apache web server may need to make changes to the source code to meet proprietary needs. For example, they may need to change how Apache transfers information over the network. Generally, they need to do something that the standard Apache configuration files don't allow them to do. These people have a heck of a lot more programming knowledge than I do.

- **Security auditing**. Another reason for downloading the source code is to review it for vulnerabilities and bugs before compiling and running it on your server. Many organizations require all software installed on their servers to be audited before being deployed publicly. If this sounds familiar, you may want to download a copy of the Apache source code to hand over to the powers that be.

- **Education**. Just like it sounds. If you're trying to learn a programming language, what better way than to use an existing application as an example? Apache has thousands of lines of code, all publicly open for viewing. It serves as an excellent educational tool for aspiring programmers.

Unless you're running an operating system that doesn't have a package manager (such as Ubuntu), you don't want to choose the source install. It's mainly there for the super techie folk. You gain some amount of geek credibility by saying you were able to compile an application from the source. Of course, you also spend much longer getting it to work than if you had just grabbed a binary install from your package manager in the first place.

The Apache source code can be found at `www.apache.org/dist/httpd/`. If you want to travel down this road, follow the process documented by the Apache group at `http://httpd.apache.org/docs/install.html#traditional`.

The Benefit of Binary Installation

OK, maybe getting the source code isn't right for you, so you've decided to do a binary install. This is a precompiled version of Apache for your operating system. Binary installs are available for Windows, Linux, most commercial versions of UNIX, and macOS X.

The benefit of the binary file is that you significantly reduce the time between downloading the Apache install and running an Apache web server. The drawback, of course, is that you completely remove the ability to customize Apache before installing it (not that you need or want to).

For this book, I will use Ubuntu as the Linux distribution of choice; however, the instructions work for any DEB-based distribution, such as Debian, Knoppix, or Raspberry Pi's Raspbian OS.

First, open your terminal and type the following. Select **Y** when asked to continue (see Figure 1-2).

```
sudo apt-get install apache2 apache2-utils
```

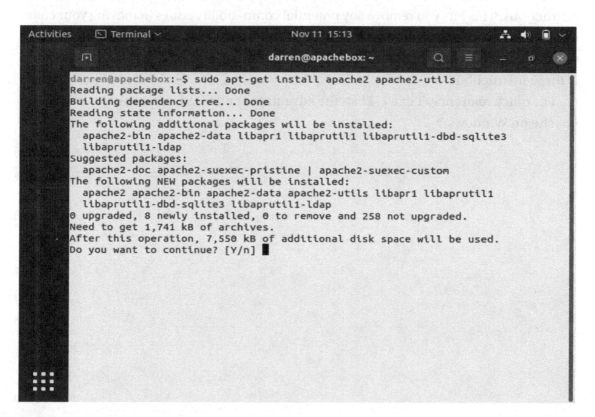

Figure 1-2. *Installing Apache on Ubuntu*

This installs Apache and some helper utilities like apachectl (which starts and stops the Apache server). Ubuntu also configures Apache to run as a service automatically, so it starts up whenever you reboot the operating system.

Once you've done that, you can skip to the "Basic Configuration" section at the end of this chapter.

Installing on Windows

Windows is the second most common choice for installing Apache, since most organizations have a ready supply of Windows servers. There are some definite advantages to using Windows (see Table 1-4); most people are already familiar with the Windows interface, so there's little time required to learn how to configure things. You may also *only* be allowed to use Windows by your organization's IT department, which removes the possibility of using Linux or macOS.

A Linux subsystem in the Windows Store allows you to follow the Linux installation instructions. This lets you remove any potential compatibility issues in moving your code from a Windows development environment to a UNIX-based one. If you go down this route (I'd recommend it!), follow the installation instructions for Linux/Ubuntu instead of these instructions.

For quick reference, Table 1-4 lists the advantages and disadvantages of installing Apache on Windows.

Table 1-4. *Advantages and Disadvantages of Using Windows*

Advantages	Disadvantages
An immediately recognizable user interface for most people	The vast majority of production web servers run on UNIX-based systems like Linux. Because of that, there's a small chance that there may be compatibility issues when you deploy code developed on a Windows system.
Smaller learning curve	Windows isn't as secure as macOS or Linux. Vulnerabilities are routinely found in Microsoft Windows, and viruses are common. This puts any sensitive information you use as part of your web development at risk of exposure, even in development environments.
Graphical tools for administration	Due to the closed development model often takes Microsoft days to release a patch after a vulnerability has been reported. Numerous other vulnerabilities may have already been found but not reported.
An existing maintenance agreement with Microsoft	System requirements for Windows are often much higher than for Linux performing the same tasks.
	Performance doesn't match Linux on the same system specifications; Linux servers offer more reliable network and file operations than Windows, using the same hardware.
	Windows machines are more prone to mysterious crashes and must be rebooted more often.
	Customization of Apache or PHP on Windows is much more complicated than on Linux or macOS.

Installing Apache Through XAMPP

I recommend using XAMPP for Windows to install Apache. XAMPP is fully open source, free of charge, and supported by a non-profit organization, Apache Friends. It is kept up to date with releases of Apache, PHP, and MariaDB (a common, open source database system based on MySQL). Other options, such as WAMP, MAMP, and AMPSS, operate similarly but may impose licensing costs. In this book, however, refer to filenames and locations in XAMPP.

You can download XAMPP at www.apachefriends.org. Follow the on-screen directions to install the software, selecting C:\XAMPP\ as the Installation folder. During the installation, keep the default options selected. At a minimum, you should install Apache and PHP because they are used later in this book.

Installing Apache as a Service in Windows

User Account Control (UAC) prevents Apache from operating as a full system service on Windows. If you want to use Apache this way, you must ensure that your account has administrator privileges and needs to either disable UAC[9] (not recommended) or run XAMPP with administrator privileges. This is done by right-clicking the **XAMPP Control Panel** icon and selecting **More ➤ Run as administrator** (see Figure 1-3).

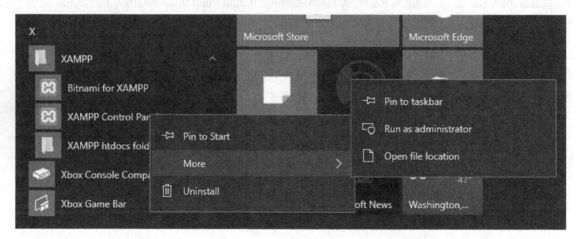

Figure 1-3. *Running XAMPP as administrator on Windows*

When the XAMPP control panel has loaded with administrator privileges, you see the option to turn on Apache (and other tools) as a service in Windows. This means it starts up whenever Windows starts up, instead of being manually turned on when you want it. Select the Apache checkbox to enable the service (see Figure 1-4).

---

[9] See https://stackoverflow.com/questions/26208848/xampp-installation-on-win-8-1-with-uac-warning

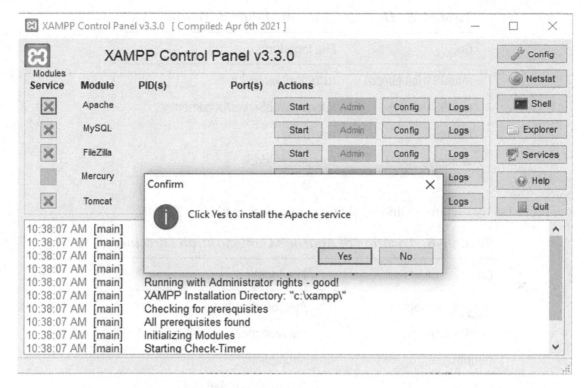

Figure 1-4. *XAMPP control panel*

Apache now starts up whenever you reboot your Windows computer.

Basic Configuration

So now that you have Apache installed, what do you do with it? The simplest configuration for Apache is one that serves up static HTML files and any linked files like graphics, CSS, or JavaScript.

Where to Put Your Website Files

When first installed, Apache specifies where it expects to find your publicly accessible website files. This directory should already exist on your computer as part of the Apache install (see Table 1-5). Something to note is that this directory is not always configured on some operating systems to allow access to non-administrator accounts.

Table 1-5. *Default Location of Public Website Files*

On...	File location
macOS (Homebrew)	/usr/local/var/www
macOS (Native)	/Library/WebServer/Documents/
Ubuntu	/var/www
Windows 10 /11	C:\xampp\htdocs

Table 1-6 lists where to find Apache's configuration files.

Table 1-6. *Location of Apache's Configuration Directory*

On...	File location
macOS (Homebrew)	/usr/local/etc/httpd
macOS (Native)	/etc/apache2
Ubuntu	/etc/apache2
Windows 10 / 11	C:\xampp\apache\conf

Configuration Directory Structure

macOS and XAMPP on Windows follow the configuration directory structure recommended by Apache (see Table 1-7), whereas Ubuntu uses a slightly different directory structure. This reflects how Apache is used differently on each operating system: macOS and Windows are used solely as individual working environments, whereas Ubuntu is often used as a server environment with several module-based options for configuration. Ubuntu needs to use a different directory structure to support adding and removing functionality through their package manager. To learn more about how Ubuntu configures Apache, refer to their documentation at `https://ubuntu.com/server/docs/web-servers-apache`.

Table 1-7. *Contents of Apache Configuration Directory*

macOS and Windows	Ubuntu Linux
[Apache configuration directory]	/etc/apache2/
|- extra (directory)	|- apache2.conf
| |- *.conf	|- conf-available
|- httpd.conf	| |- *.conf
|- magic	|- conf-enabled (directory)
|- mime-types	| |- *.conf (symbolic links to ../conf-available)
|- original (directory)	|- envvars
| |- extra (directory)	|- magic
| | |- *.conf	|- mods-available (directory)
| |- httpd.conf	| |- *.conf
	|- mods-enabled (directory)
	| |- *.conf (symbolic links to ../mods-available)
	|- ports.conf
	|- sites-available (directory)
	| |- *.conf
	|- sites-enabled (directory)
	| |- *.conf (symbolic links to ../sites-available)

In this book, I focus on the macOS and Windows directory structures when talking about configuration. Though I recommend you follow Ubuntu's provided directory structure on Linux, you *can* work outside of that structure to follow the examples in this book. Apache is flexible that way!

Now let's review what those configuration files do.

httpd.conf/apache2.conf

All of Apache's basic configuration is handled in the httpd.conf file, located in the directory indicated for your operating system. This is a text file that can be edited using any plain text editor or code editing tool and contains a *lot* of configuration instructions called directives, which you'll learn more about in Chapter 2.

The default httpd.conf installed with Apache contains many more directives than you need; several directives and examples are commented out within the `httpd.conf` configuration file. This is done by placing a # at the beginning of the line. These commented directives come in very handy. For example, let's say you need to load the `mod_userdir` module, which allows your users to maintain their web pages on your server. Instead of trying to figure out what the proper name of the module is, you can just remove the comment character. All the directives discussed in the next chapter are in `httpd.conf`, unless specified otherwise.

mime.types

The `mime.types` configuration file is Apache's Rosetta Stone. The contents of the `mime.types` file matches file extensions to content types. For example, HTML files have the following entry in the `mime.types` configuration file.

```
text/html      htm html
```

This tells Apache (and the browser loading the page) that files on the server with the extensions `.htm` or `.html` should be treated as HTML files. Likewise, you might see this entry for PNG files, which lets Apache know that files with a `.png` extension should be treated as binary rather than text.

```
image/png      png
```

If you need to add a new file type, this is the place to do it. I discuss it a little more in the "Adding New File Types" section in Chapter 2.

Configuring a Default Site

A default site is already configured for you when you install Apache. But I find the location configured by the Apache installer is often inconvenient to get to in your file browser and sometimes has restricted permissions that require you to access administrative privileges to add or edit files.

If you were to visit `http://localhost` in your browser, you'd see something like Figure 1-5. The contents of this file, on macOS, can be found in `/usr/local/var/www/index.html` (this file is created as part of the Apache installation). Try editing this file and reloading it in your browser!

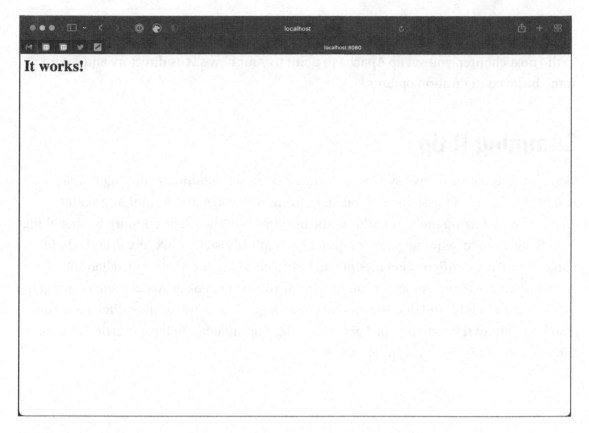

Figure 1-5. *Apache's default website*

When setting things up, I like to reconfigure Apache to point to a different, more easily accessible directory on my computer. For example, on macOS or Linux, I usually create a directory called `sites` in my home directory (`/home/darren/sites/` on Linux, and `/Users/darren/sites` on macOS) that contains all the projects I'm working on. On Windows, I create `C:\sites\` to store my projects. This lets me later configure Apache for multiple virtual host sites that I can place in this directory, such as the following.

- `http://project.local` stored in `/home/darren/sites/project/`

- `http://funtoy.local` stored in `/home/darren/sites/funtoy/`

- `http://skunkworks.local` stored in `/home/darren/sites/workproject/`

Make your own `sites` directory, and jot the location down in your favorite notes app. You reference this directory in the httpd.conf or apache2.conf file later in this book. In the next chapter, you set up Apache to point to your new `sites` directory and set up some basic configuration options.

Summing It Up

Congratulations! You now have a solid foundation of server fundamentals and Apache installed in its most basic form. If you do nothing else, you can start building static websites and making them available to the browser. You should be comfortable installing Apache anywhere, whether your computer or a cloud-hosted Linux server, and where you can find the configuration files needed to customize your Apache installation.

Chapter 2 explains Apache's configuration. You set up a basic Apache site pointing to `http://localhost/` and develop an understanding of the configuration directives. You also learn about the structure of Apache's configuration files and local overrides through the `.htaccess` file. See you there!

CHAPTER 2

Configuration Essentials

This chapter teaches you how to set up a basic Apache instance on your local computer (localhost). To get there, I cover the structure of Apache's configuration and commonly used Apache directives, which are commands Apache uses to define its configuration. You also learn about local overrides through the `.htaccess` file.

By the end of this chapter, you have a basic running website at `http://localhost` that you can use for developing basic HTML/CSS-based websites.

Apache uses two sets of configuration files. The first set is server-level and is contained mostly in the `httpd.conf` file. The second set of configuration files is a directory-level configuration file and supersedes any server-level configuration (if allowed).

Before you begin, back up the original configuration files into a different directory. You'll thank me for this later.

How Apache's Configuration Is Structured

One of the reasons Apache is such a lean server application is that its many directives (discussed later in the chapter) are broken out into a modular system that breaks functionality into several library files. These files are only accessed when Apache needs them, so Apache doesn't have to store the information in memory until it's needed. These libraries are called modules in Apache.

Apache comes with a wide variety of modules, including virtual hosting, authentication, scripting engines, and URL rewriting. By default, quite a few modules are enabled in Apache because they're crucial to the day-to-day operations of your website (for example, the logging module `mod_log_config` is enabled by default to provide logging of events from your web server).

Apache's modules don't follow a set naming scheme but seem to use one of two conventions most of the time. The most common naming convention is `mod_`

© Darren James Harkness 2022
D. J. Harkness, *Apache Essentials*, https://doi.org/10.1007/978-1-4842-8324-0_2

modulename. For example, the module that governs CGI applications is named mod_cgi. Almost all the modules developed and released by the Apache Group follow this convention.

The second most common way to name Apache modules takes its inspiration from Perl. Perl modules are often named along the lines of Application::Function. An example would be Apache::RandomImage (a module that randomly displays images in a directory). For most people, the modules included with Apache by default are more than enough to handle a website's daily needs. You should only need to add modules for scripting languages or specific programming functionality (image manipulation libraries, for example). Apache uses the Perl module format, which gives it access to thousands of modules.

The modules in Table 2-1 are installed by default in Apache. They're included by using the LoadModule directive inside of the httpd.conf configuration file. Other modules are loaded by default, but I wanted to call these out as useful ones.

Table 2-1. *Useful Default Apache Modules*

Module Name	What It Does	Associated Directives
auth_ basic_ module	Apache uses this module to provide basic authentication of sites Apache is configured to serve.	AuthGroupFile AuthUserFile AuthAuthoritative
mod_ access	This module allows for access control by IP address.	Allow Deny Order
mod_alias	This module allows you to map directories outside your DocumentRoot as part of your web documents. For example, you could create a shared cgi-bin directory at /usr/lib/cgi-bin (or C:\cgi-bin) and alias it to www.domain.com/cgi-bin.	Alias AliasMatch Redirect RedirectMatch RedirectTemp RedirectPermanent ScriptAlias ScriptAliasMatch

(*continued*)

Table 2-1. (*continued*)

Module Name	What It Does	Associated Directives
mod_ autoindex	This module automatically creates an index of a requested directory if no DirectoryIndex file is set or found within the directory.	AddAlt AddAltByEncoding AddAltByType AddDescription AddIcon AddIconByEncoding AddIconByType DefaultIcon FancyIndexing HeaderName IndexIgnore IndexOptions IndexOrderDefault ReadmeName
mod_cgi	Apache uses this module to run any CGI script or file with a MIME type of application/x-http-cgi.	ScriptLog ScriptLogLength ScriptBuffer
mod_dir	This module works with the DirectoryIndex directive to automatically tell Apache what files to load when a directory is requested. For example, if you configure the DirectoryIndex directive as index.html, the index.html file is loaded when a browser requests www.domain.com/somedir/. If this isn't enabled, the browser displays a file listing of all documents within the folder.	DirectoryIndex
mod_env	This module allows scripts to access Apache's environment variables, which track information such as the current client's IP address, browser, referrer, and so on.	PassEnv SetEnv UnsetEnv

(*continued*)

Table 2-1. (*continued*)

Module Name	What It Does	Associated Directives
mod_log_config	This module allows for the CustomLog directive (see Chapter 7 for more information).	CookieLog CustomLog LogFormat TransferLog
mod_mime	This module determines how certain documents are to be displayed. For example, an HTML document is displayed differently than a simple text document.	AddCharset AddEncoding AddHandler AddLanguage AddType DefaultLanguage ForceType RemoveEncoding RemoveHandler RemoveType SetHandler TypesConfig

In addition to the default Apache modules mentioned earlier, I suggest enabling the `mod_rewrite` module, which is often used by content management systems to provide human-readable URLs.

Where Do I Find Modules?

As you've already seen, Apache installs almost all the modules you need. If you need something that the Apache Group doesn't provide, there are two places you can go.

The first is the Apache Group's documentation, which has a list of modules developed by the Apache Group and included for use with Apache. It's not a long list, but you might find what you need there. You can find the list of included modules at `http://httpd.apache.org/docs/mod/index-bytype.html`.

If the list of included modules doesn't contain what you need, you can go to Wikipedia's list of Apache modules. For example, you might want an Apache module that allows you to run .NET on your Apache server. None of Apache's official modules support this, but the Mono project developed a third-party module that does support it.[1]

Installing Modules

If you find an Apache module that you'd like to install, it's a relatively simple process to install and configure a module.

In Apache, you use the `LoadModule` directive to dynamically load modules. The `LoadModule` directive doesn't require modules to be compiled against Apache ahead of time. It uses precompiled binary files that are distributed with the module.

The `LoadModule` directive takes two options. The first option gives the name of the module as it is known to Apache. Most modules tell you what their suggested name is in their documentation. I'd recommend sticking to their suggestions. The second option tells Apache where it can find the module's library file. In Linux and macOS X, this file has a .so extension. In Windows, this file has a `.dll` extension.

A typical `LoadModule` directive looks like the following.

```
LoadModule include_module modules/mod_include.so
```

Adding File Types

This module allows you to specify outside of the `mime.types` configuration file, how Apache should handle certain file types. For example, Chapter 3 discusses adding PHP to your server. As part of that configuration, you must tell Apache how to handle files with the `.php` extension. Let's add a line like this to your `httpd.conf`.

```
AddType application/x-http-php     .php
```

---

[1]`www.mono-project.com/docs/web/mod_mono/`

Configuring Modules

Many modules have their own configuration directives that Apache won't understand if the module fails to load. As a result, it's a good idea to use conditional `<IfModule>` sections within your `httpd.conf` so that you can include these directives safely; if the module doesn't load, Apache skips them entirely.

These sections only load directives if Apache can find and load the module to which they're attached. An example of this is included in the sample `httpd.conf` installed with Apache.

```
<IfModule dir_module>
    DirectoryIndex index.html
</IfModule>
```

All About Directives

Directives are what Apache calls its various configuration options. These are commands used within Apache's configuration files to configure various aspects of the server. Each directive takes up a single line and generally follows the same format.

Directive Configuration

For example, if you want to configure the location where Apache can find the site's HTML files, you would use the `DocumentRoot` directive and supply a path.

DocumentRoot /var/www

There are, quite literally, hundreds of directives available in Apache and many more added in Apache's modules. However, this chapter only focuses on a few of the more commonly used ones, as outlined in Table 2-2.

Table 2-2. *Commonly Used Configuration Directives*

Directive	Description	Example
ServerName		
Listen	It tells the server to listen on a specific port for requests. The common ports are 80 (http://) and 443 (https://).	Listen 80
DocumentRoot	It specifies the directory Apache should look at for publicly accessible files. Apache needs read and execute permissions on this directory.	DocumentRoot /var/www
<Directory>	It starts a configuration section that allows you to specify directives for your DocumentRoot (and any other directories accessible via Apache).	<Directory /var/www> AllowOverride All Options FollowSymLinks MultiViews Order allow, deny Allow from all </Directory>
Options	This configures which Apache feature are available to the directory.	Options Indexes, FollowSymLinks
AllowOverride	It allows local overrides of a directory's Apache configuration through the use of a .htaccess file. You can specify All, None, or specific groups of directives.	AllowOverrideAll
ErrorLog	This configures the location of the error log.	ErrorLog /usr/local/var/log/ httpd/dev.localerror.log
LogFormat	It defines the formats used by the access log.	LogFormat "%h %l %u %t \"%r\" %>s %O" common

(continued)

Table 2-2. (*continued*)

Directive	Description	Example
\<VirtualHost\>	This creates a site-specific configuration in Apache, separate from the default configuration.	\<VirtualHost *:80\> ServerAdmin hello@ apachebook.com DocumentRoot "/Users/ darren/code/apachebook. local" ServerName shipton.local ErrorLog "/usr/local/var/ log/httpd/apachebook. local-error_log" Customlog "/usr/ local/var/log/httpd/ apachebook.local-access_log" common \</VirtualHost\>

Let's learn more about how to use these directives.

Configuring Your Primary Apache Site

Remember in the previous chapter, where I asked you to write down the location of your code directory? Here's where you use that. When first installed, Apache looks for the HTML files it serves in one of the directories listed in Table 2-3.

Table 2-3. *Default Location of Public Website Files*

On...	File Location
macOS (Homebrew)	/usr/local/var/www
macOS (Native)	/var/www
Ubuntu	/var/www
Windows 10/11	C:\xampp\htdocs

But, as I said in the previous chapter, those locations can be hard to remember and sometimes protected by system privileges. Let's create a new place, called sites, to put the HTML files in your home directory.

Creating the New Directory

Open your terminal and enter the following command in either macOS or Linux.

```
cd ~/
```

This navigates you to your home directory on the system. In Windows, you want to get to the root of the C drive. You'd instead enter

```
cd \
```

Now that you're in the right place, it's time to make your sites directory. Type the following command.

```
mkdir sites
```

followed by this command to change into the new directory.

```
cd sites
```

Finally, you want to create a directory for the primary site. Follow the preceding two steps (mkdir and cd) to create a directory called primary.

You end up with the information listed in Table 2-4 (replacing *darren* with your username on the computer for macOS and Linux installations).

Table 2-4. *Location of Primary Code Directory*

On...	File Location
macOS	/Users/darren/sites/primary
Ubuntu	/home/darren/sites/primary
Windows 10/11	C:\sites\primary

Updating Your Apache Configuration

Although you can configure Apache for multiple domains, there is always a primary site to which the server defaults. At the end of Chapter 1, I talked about creating a sites directory that's easier for you to manage than the default Apache /var/www directory.

Updating the Location of Your Website's Files

The first thing you need to do is define where Apache's looks for the files used by your website. This is done through the DocumentRoot directive, which is found in the httpd. conf configuration file.

Search for **DocumentRoot**, and change the existing directory to your new primary site directory. For example, on macOS, the following would be set.

```
DocumentRoot /Users/darren/sites
```

In Windows, you usually have to enclose the path to your web documents within quotations. It would look something like the following.

```
DocumentRoot "C:/sites/primary"
```

After configuring the main document root directory for Apache, you need to specify options for it by creating a <Directory> entry. This sets the actual configuration of your website within Apache, and controls what access files on your website have.

```
<Directory /Users/darren/sites/primary>
    Options Indexes Includes FollowSymLinks MultiViews
    AllowOverride All
    Order allow,deny
    Allow from all
</Directory>
```

This can be broken down pretty easily. In the <Directory> directive, you need to specify the directory you're configuring. Since you want to configure the main site, you should match the DocumentRoot directory, /Users/darren/sites/primary. If you want to specify options for a different directory, let's say /cgi-bin, you would add another section, like the following.

```
<Directory /Users/darren/sites/primary/cgi-bin>
    Options Indexes Includes FollowSymLinks ExecCGI MultiViews
```

```
    AllowOverride All
</Directory>
```

This section would allow CGI files to be executed in the /cgi-bin directory, but not within the rest of your website. This allows you to contain all script files to a single directory, making it easier to audit what scripts are running on your Apache server.

When you configure a directory, you also configure all its subdirectories. So, when you make changes to /Users/darren/sites/primary, the changes would also be applied to /Users/darren/sites/primary/images. To give special configurations to individual subdirectories within your main DocumentRoot, you must create separate <Directory> entries for each.

Directory Options

After you've told Apache which directory you want to set options for, you need to tell it which options to configure the directory with. Table 2-5 lists the many options you can set on a directory.

Table 2-5. *Available Settings for the Options Directive*

Option	Description	Should I use it?
All	Enables all options except MultiViews. It is the default setting.	If you're looking for a quick way to configure a directory and are not concerned about performance or security, then yes. Otherwise, specify your options manually.
AllowOverride	Specifies which directives an .htaccess file stored in the site's directories can override. The default setting is None, which prevents any overrides of the Apache site's configuration. Individual directives can be specified for overriding, or All can be provided, which allows all eligible directives to be overridden.	Some web applications may require the ability for a .htaccess file to override the Apache configuration to function properly. This is common in many content management systems.

(continued)

Table 2-5. (*continued*)

Option	Description	Should I use it?
ExecCGI	Allows CGI files to be executed in the directory. This should only be enabled for directories containing scripts because enabling it for all directories causes Apache to take a hit on its performance.	You should use this only for directories that contain CGI files. Note that you do not need to use this setting for PHP or Node.js files within a directory.
FollowSymLinks	If this is enabled, the server follows symbolic links within a directory. Symbolic links are similar to Windows shortcuts; they point to other files or directories within a UNIX system. This option is ignored if used within a <Location> directive.	Yes. This allows you to set up shortcuts to files and directories without duplicating documents on your system. This is a side benefit because you only need to edit the original file, and all symbolic links are automatically updated.
Indexes	If no documents matching the ones specified in the DocumentIndex directive are found (index.html, for example), Apache returns a formatted directory listing of the requested URL.	This option can be enabled or disabled, depending on the level of security that you want on your Apache server. If this option is enabled, it shows users a listing of the files within a directory. Though this is fine for most applications, you may not want it for others (for example, a directory that contains script files). If this option isn't enabled, a request for a directory that doesn't contain a DocumentIndex file return a 403 forbidden error.

(continued)

Table 2-5. (*continued*)

Option	Description	Should I use it?
MultiViews	The MultiViews directive searches for files matching the requested file. For example, if a requested file doesn't exist on the server, such as index. html, Apache display the closest match before reporting a 404 not found error, such as index.htm.	This is recommended so that you can catch any mild typos made by people requesting URLs.
SymLinksIfOwnerMatch	It is identical to the FollowSymLinks option but only follows the symbolic link if it's owned by the same user on the system as the original directory. If the same user does not own the symlink, the symbolic link is not followed.	It's a good idea to enable this option if you want to preserve security within your system. For example, enabling this option is a good idea if you allow users on your system to have their own websites through user directories.

Configuring Your Primary Index File

When loading a directory request, Apache looks for the index.html file. To change its default behavior, you must use the DirectoryIndex directive. For example, if you wanted the server to load welcome.htm instead of index.html when a directory request is received, you would use the following.

```
DirectoryIndex welcome.htm
```

DirectoryIndex is often used in the context of .htaccess but can also be specified within a <Directory> section in the httpd.conf configuration file. For now, let's keep this as index.html. You'll change this in Chapter 3 when you configure Apache for scripting languages like PHP and Node.js.

```
DirectoryIndex index.html
```

Configuring Logging

Apache makes use of two primary directives for logging: `CustomLog` and `ErrorLog`. `CustomLog` specifies the location and format of the general access log for a site, which records all requested URLs. `ErrorLog` records only errors encountered when trying to start or restart Apache or attempting to execute scripts such as CGI or PHP files.

When installing Apache, it adds a default configuration for both directives. For now, you can leave this alone. In Chapter 6, you learn how to configure logging in more detail, which is useful for separating log files for multiple virtual domains.

Using .htaccess Files

If the `AllowOverride` directive is set to anything other than None, you can specify certain configuration options at the directory level through the `.htaccess` file. This file is often used for rewriting URLs, authenticating users in a protected directory, or specifying error documents for a site.

The directives contained within the `.htaccess` file precede over those in the `httpd.conf` configuration file, and apply to all subdirectories contained within.

The following is an example of a `.htaccess` file configuring basic authentication and setting up clean URLs that redirect everything to a parameter or `index.php`.

```
DirectoryIndex index.html index.htm
AuthName "Site Statistics...."
AuthType Basic
AuthUserFile /home/darren/sites/stats/.htpasswd
require valid-user
<IfModule mod_rewrite.c>
    RewriteEngine On
    # Enable clean URLs
    RewriteCond %{REQUEST_FILENAME} !-f
    RewriteCond %{REQUEST_FILENAME} !-d
    RewriteCond %{REQUEST_URI} !^/(favicon\.ico|apple-touch-icon.*\.
    png)$ [NC]
    RewriteRule (.+) index.php?p=$1 [QSA,L]
</IfModule>
```

Other Configuration Options You Should Know

The preceding gets you started with an Apache installation. However, there are several other common configuration options that you likely come across and should be familiar with as you build out your websites.

Rewriting URLs

In a redesign situation, you often need to move the contents of one directory to another. On a mechanical basis, this is pretty easy and doesn't pose a problem. You just copy the files from one location to another. You only need to change your HTML so that users can find the new location.

One tried and true method used by webmasters from time immemorial is to replace the old HTML file with one that tells the user that the file has been moved to a new location, followed by a request to update their bookmarks to match the new location.

But this causes a couple of problems. First, the user is inconvenienced since they must go an extra step to find the content they were looking for. And some may not understand immediately that the content has been moved; they'll just see it isn't there. The second problem is much more serious, however. Search engines won't follow your links. They simply see that the content has changed and that it no longer matches the search terms the page used to be associated with.

Apache supplies an alternative in the `mod_rewrite` module. This module allows you to create custom rules to rewrite document requests in a way that automatically forwards the user through to the right place. The `mod_rewrite` module works by capturing a request and comparing it against the Apache configuration file. If a match is found, it processes the rule and redirects the user to the supplied location.

Apache's rewrite module can be configured in its main configuration file or at the domain level through a `.htaccess` file (if you allow local overrides). It uses two main directives: `RewriteCond`, which lets you specify conditions for the reset, and `RewriteRule`, which defines a specific element to redirect. Both directives understand regular expressions,[2] making them very powerful for managing multiple redirects with

---

[2] If you're unfamiliar with regular expressions (also known as *regex*), they are patterns that you can use within many UNIX-based systems. They let you find strings that match a set of conditions. There are several resources, such as `https://regexr.com` and `https://regex101.com`, that can help you to learn, build, and test regular expressions.

fewer configuration lines. A section of rewrite rules begins with a single `RewriteEngine On` directive, which tells Apache to enable the module and process the following directives using it.

Table 2-6 presents the directives you commonly use with the `Rewrite` module.

Table 2-6. *Rewrite Directives*

Directive	Explanation
RewriteBase	This directive sets a base URL for the following conditions and rules defined.
RewriteCond	It defines conditions for the following RewriteRule. You can set multiple conditions for an individual RewriteRule. If the conditions are not met, the associated RewriteRule is not executed.
RewriteEngine	It turns the Apache rewriting module on and off. By default, the rewriting engine is off, which means you need to include RewriteEngine On at the start of any configuration section, including RewriteRule.
RewriteRule	This is where you define your URL rewrite. You can use regular expressions, and you can rewrite to URLs on the same domain or a separate domain.

Let's go through a couple of examples that you will likely encounter.

Using URL Slugs

Most modern content management systems use URL slugs, which are human-readable URLs for their content pages. This makes it easier for people to remember how to get back to a specific page. It has a strong positive effect on search engine optimization since the URLs contain additional contextual information about the page contents. For example, a URL slug translates `https://mydomain.com/index.php?id=4142` to a much more friendly `https://mydomain.com/services/user-experience/`.

Here's an example from Craft CMS, which captures any directory passed through to Apache and redirects it quietly as an HTTP query parameter to `index.php`.

```
<IfModule mod_rewrite.c>
    RewriteEngine On
    # Send would-be 404 requests to Craft
    RewriteCond %{REQUEST_FILENAME} !-f
    RewriteCond %{REQUEST_FILENAME} !-d
```

```
    RewriteCond %{REQUEST_URI} !^/(favicon\.ico|apple-touch-icon.*\.
    png)$ [NC]
    RewriteRule (.+) index.php?p=$1 [QSA,L]
</IfModule>
```

Table 2-7 goes through this example line by line.

Table 2-7. *Breakdown of Conditional Rewrites*

Directive	Explanation
<IfModule mod_ rewrite.c>	If the Rewrite module isn't enabled or installed, you want Apache to skip this section so that it doesn't fail with an error when it's loading. Of course, that means that the directives contained within this section do not redirect traffic.
RewriteEngine On	Turn on Apache's RewriteEngine.
# Send would-be 404 requests to Craft	This is a comment and is ignored by Apache when reading through this section. Comments are exceptionally useful in larger configuration files so that you or the person editing this configuration file have some context around what's been configured and why.
RewriteCond %{REQUEST_ FILENAME} !-f	It tells Apache to ignore this RewriteRule if a file already exists at this URL. For example, you want this rule to be ignored for all linked assets on the server, like CSS, JavaScript, or image files. Let's say you have a banner image linked to at https://mydomain.com/ assets/img/welcome.png. When Apache reads this set of RewriteRules, it reads what's in the %{REQUEST_FILENAME} variable, /assets/img/ welcome.png, and see if it exists as a file on the system (at /var/www/ html/image/welcome.png). You're creating a condition that says you want to rewrite if it is *not* an existing file, which you specify with ! (the not character) and -f (a flag in Apache that signifies files). Because the /assets/img/welcome.png file exists on the server, Apache records the condition as not being met and stop processing this rule.

(continued)

Table 2-7. (*continued*)

Directive	Explanation
RewriteCond %{REQUEST_ FILENAME} !-d	It is identical to the previous directive, but it is used for directories (the -d flag). This is used when the website uses URL slugs but has a separate administrative set of scripts. An example of this would be WordPress, which contains a wp-admin directory on the web server.
RewriteCond %{REQUEST_URI} !^/(favicon\. ico|apple- touch-icon.*\. png)$ [NC]	This condition instructs Apache to ignore two specific files: favicon.ico and apple-touch-icon.png (and some derivatives). There are two notable things in this RewriteRule to pay attention to. First, you're using the !(not) character along with a regular expression, which is indicated by the ^ character: ^/(favicon\.ico|apple-touch-icon.*.png)$. Second is the [NC] flag, which is an interaction to Apache to ignore upper and lower case when evaluating the URL against this condition. The combination of the two cause Apache to ignore any URLs such as the following when considering rewrites: https://mydomain.com/favicon.ico https://mydomain.com/Favicon.ico https://mydomain.com/apple-touch-icon.2x.png https://mydomain.com/apple-touch-icon.3x.png Putting this rewrite condition into human speech, you'd end up with this: "if the URL does not contain /favicon.ico or /apple-touch-icon.*.png"

(*continued*)

Table 2-7. (*continued*)

Directive	Explanation
RewriteRule (.+) index. php?p=$1 [QSA,L]	It is the rule that the preceding conditions apply. You commonly see several groups of RewriteCond and RewriteRule in an Apache configuration. (.+) is a regular expression used as a global wildcard. Everything after the first slash following the domain in the URL is saved as a variable, which is accessed by the $1 in the next section. Now that you know what you need to rewrite, it's time to tell Apache where it's rewriting to. This is done with index.php?p=$1. This redirects any URL that isn't an existing file or directory to a query parameter of the index.php file. For example, https://mydomain.com/articles would redirect to https://mydomain.com/index.php?p=articles. Finally, you pass some additional flags in square brackets to let Apache know how to continue. The first of these is QSA. This tells Apache to combine the old URL with the new one provided. The second flag, L, tells Apache to stop considering RewriteRules if it has met this one's conditions. If no L flag is supplied, Apache continues to evaluate the URL against subsequent rewrite rules, which may cause conflicts and a nasty error message.
</IfModule>	It completes the set of RewriteRules and closes the section opened by the <IfModule mod_rewrite.c> opening directive. If the </IfModule> directive does not appear, Apache reports an error and prevents itself from starting.

Putting the information from this table into human-readable language, you'd get the following.

"If the URL is not a file or a directory, and not a file named either favicon.ico or some variation of apple-touch-icon.png, redirect the full URL to index.php as the value for the p parameter, then stop evaluating rules."

Updating the URL for an Existing Page

It's common as your website grows older that its URL structure change. For example, your site may have started as a blog, storing each entry under a date-based URL structure like https://mydomain.com/2021/12/25/interesting-topic. Perhaps as you grow as an online professional, you want to convert those blog entries to articles, using a structure like https://mydomain.com/articles/interesting-topic. You've probably built up a strong search engine for those old blog articles, which you don't want to lose.

You need a way to let the search engines know the content has moved so that it doesn't significantly affect your search engine traffic. Of course, you also have dozens of blog entries that need to move over. You could write out an individual

```
<IfModule mod_rewrite.c>
  RewriteEngine On

  # Redirect old blog entries to new articles
  RewriteRule ^(\d{4})/(\d{2})/(\d{2})/? articles/$4 [R=301,L]

</IfModule>
```

Table 2-8 goes through this example line by line.

Table 2-8. *Breakdown of a Rewrite Configuration Using Regular Expressions*

Directive	Explanation
<IfModule mod_ rewrite.c>	If the Rewrite module isn't enabled or installed, you want Apache to skip this section so that it doesn't fail with an error when it's loading. Of course, that means that the directives contained within this section do not redirect traffic.
RewriteEngine On	Turn on Apache's RewriteEngine.
RewriteRule ^(\d{4})/(\d{2})/ (\d{2})/? / articles/$4 [R=301,L]	This RewriteRule uses a regular expression to capture anything using a YYYY/MM/DD URL structure. It also adds two flags to the rule. The first, R=301, supplies an HTTP 301 error code along with the redirect. This lets search engines know that the old URL has been permanently moved to the new URL. The second flag, L, tells Apache to stop processing the URL against further RewriteRules.
</IfModule>	It completes the set of RewriteRules and closes the section opened by the <IfModule mod_rewrite.c> opening directive. If the </IfModule> directive does not appear, Apache reports an error and prevents itself from starting.

Putting the information from this table into human-readable language, you'd get the following.

"If the URL matches a pattern of four digits, a slash, two digits, another slash, and two more digits, then send the browser to a new URL that starts with `/articles/`. Add back any portions of the URL after that pattern is met as a string after `/articles/` and then stop evaluating rules."

Fixing a Trailing Slash

One of the most common uses of the rewrite rule is to fix the "trailing slash problem." The trailing slash problem can be summarized like this: By default, Apache treats all incoming requests as file requests unless they have a trailing slash.

Let's look at an example. A user requests `https://www.domain.com/about`. Apache looks for a file called about in the site folder but ignores directories with the same name. If a file called *about* doesn't exist, but a directory named *about* does, Apache report a `404 file not found` error to the user. If the user requests `https://www.domain.com/about/`, Apache finds the *about* directory, then loads the configured `DocumentIndex` file for it. This can be exceptionally frustrating for users and developers alike since, from a human perspective, there should be no difference between `https://www.domain.com/about` and `https://www.domain.com/about/`.

This is generally a condition handled by most modern CMS, but you may still run across it from time to time.

Here's an example of how you can work around this using Apache's RewriteEngine.

```
<IfModule mod_rewrite.c>
    RewriteEngine On
    # Redirect Trailing Slashes If Not A Folder...
    RewriteCond %{REQUEST_FILENAME} !-d
    RewriteCond %{REQUEST_URI} (.+)/$
    RewriteRule ^$ %1
</IfModule>
```

Table 2-9 goes through this line by line.

Table 2-9. *Breakdown of a Conditional Rewrite to Remove a Trailing Slash*

Directive	Explanation
`<IfModule mod_` `rewrite.c>`	If the Rewrite module isn't enabled or installed, you want Apache to skip this section so that it doesn't fail with an error when it's loading. Of course, that means that the directives contained within this section do not redirect traffic.
`RewriteEngine On`	Turn on Apache's RewriteEngine.

`# Redirect`
`Trailing Slashes`
`If Not A`
`Folder...`
	It is a comment ignored by Apache when reading through the section. Comments are exceptionally useful in larger configuration files so that you or the person editing this configuration file have some context around what's been configured and why.

`RewriteCond`
`%{REQUEST_`
`FILENAME} !-d`
	This condition ensures that a directory doesn't already exist. If it does, Apache marks the condition as not met and stops evaluating the URL against this rule.

`RewriteCond`
`%{REQUEST_URI}`
`(.+)/$`
	This checks to see if there is a slash at the end of the URL (e.g., `https://`
	`mydomain.com/trailing/`). If it does not, Apache mark the condition as not met and stops evaluating the URL against this rule.

`RewriteRule` `^(.*)/($) $1 [L]`	This rule removes the trailing slash from the URL. It also contains the L flag, which instructs Apache to stop evaluating the URL against further RewriteRules.

Putting the preceding into human-readable language, you'd get the following.

"If the URL is not a file or a directory, and contains a forward slash at the end of the URL, remove the slash from the end of the URL and stop evaluating rules."

Creating Custom Error Messages

By default, Apache opens a very plain page when an error is encountered. As you can see in the following figure, the default Apache error message gives little detail about the error.

If Apache is not configured to provide an error document, you see an unfriendly screen like the one shown in Figure 2-1, or even worse, simply a blank white page. This is disruptive on live websites because it takes the user outside your organization's branding while giving them no real solution or way out of the error.

Figure 2-1. *Standard Apache error page*

As you can see, the error message isn't very descriptive or helpful for the end user; there's no explanation of why the user got the error and no way for the user to find what he or she was looking for. It's also a showstopper for search engines, whose spiders are stopped dead in their tracks by the 404 message and do not continue to catalog your site. Figure 2-2 is a good example of a useful 404 error message on Jakob Nielsen's site at `https://www.nngroup.com`.

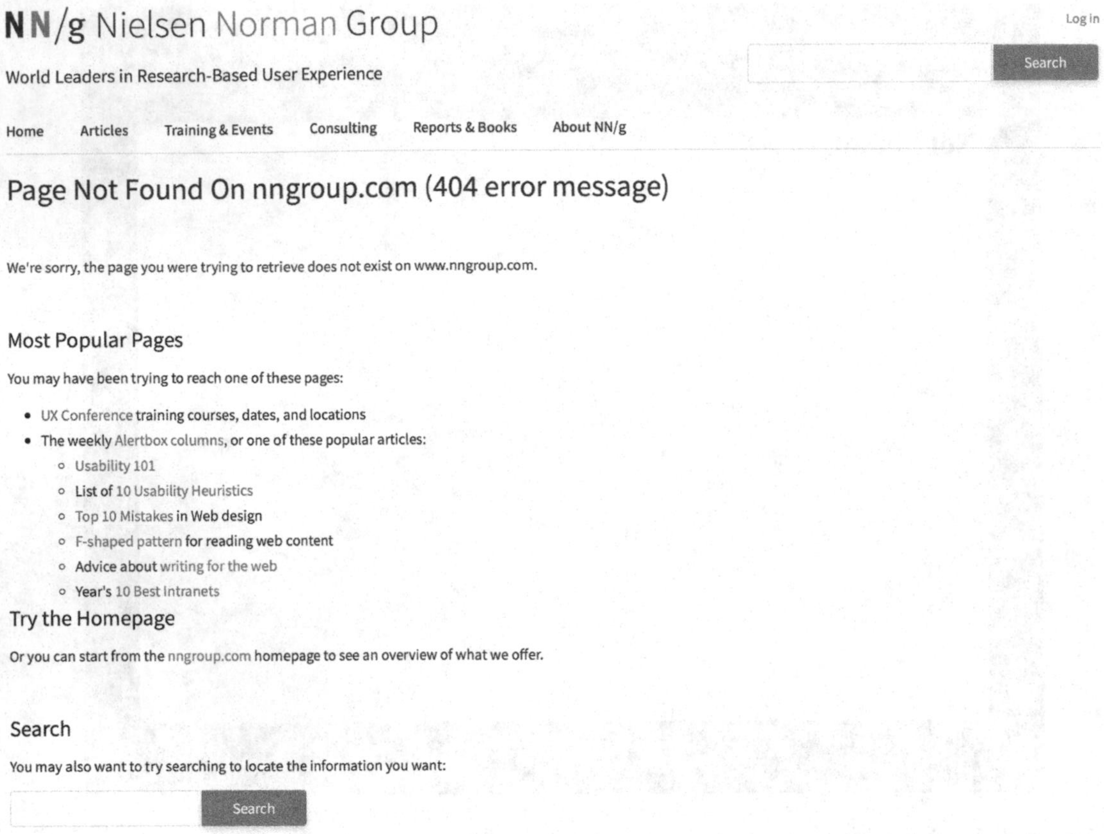

NN/g Nielsen Norman Group

World Leaders in Research-Based User Experience

Home   Articles   Training & Events   Consulting   Reports & Books   About NN/g

Log in

Search

Page Not Found On nngroup.com (404 error message)

We're sorry, the page you were trying to retrieve does not exist on www.nngroup.com.

Most Popular Pages

You may have been trying to reach one of these pages:

- UX Conference training courses, dates, and locations
- The weekly Alertbox columns, or one of these popular articles:
    - Usability 101
    - List of 10 Usability Heuristics
    - Top 10 Mistakes in Web design
    - F-shaped pattern for reading web content
    - Advice about writing for the web
    - Year's 10 Best Intranets

Try the Homepage

Or you can start from the nngroup.com homepage to see an overview of what we offer.

Search

You may also want to try searching to locate the information you want:

Search

Figure 2-2. *A customized error page*

As you can see, the page outlines how you may have arrived at this page by explaining the common mistakes made on the site. It then goes on to display the most popular pages on the website along with a link to the home page, so you can move quickly to the content you were expecting. Finally, the page provides search functionality so that you can search for content that isn't covered by what I discussed.

This is handled in Apache through the `ErrorDocument` directive. This directive lets you specify HTML files the web server should load if an error is encountered when trying to load a URL.

Table 2-10 lists a few common HTTP error codes that you want to account for.

Table 2-10. *Common HTTP Error Codes*

Error Code	Description
401	Not authorized. This error code is used when someone attempts to access a directory protected by a username and password.
403	Forbidden. The user has requested a URL that Apache doesn't have access to. This is usually a file permissions problem.
404	Not Found. The user has requested a URL that doesn't exist on the web server.
500	Internal server error. It is one of Apache's most vague and frustrating error codes because it covers a wide range of problems. However, this is commonly caused by a scripting error. I go into this more in Chapter 6.

ErrorDocument Syntax

Error documents are handled in the following format.

```
ErrorDocument <error number> <file to display>
```

To load the /errors/404.php file when the server encounters a 404 error, you would place the following within your httpd.conf.

```
ErrorDocument 404 /errors/404.php
```

Redirecting to External Error Documents

You can also redirect users to external error documents in the ErrorDocument directive. This is most useful for the 401 and 403 errors, for which users aren't allowed access to the requested URL.

For example, if you're running an employee extranet at https://employees.domain.com, and you're employing Apache's authentication module, you can have failed logins redirected to https://www.domain.com/errors/401.php. The syntax would look like the following.

```
ErrorDocument 401 https://www.domain.com/errors/401.php
```

Authenticating Users Through Apache

Apache offers basic authentication for users on your website, which lets you password-protect directories on your web server. It can be a very useful feature for employee- or member-only sections of your website and is used by most web developers.

Basic authentication is *basic*. There's no encryption offered through basic authentication, which means that the username and password, as well as the information contained within the protected directory, travel as plain text through the Internet. Although this lack of encryption doesn't pose a problem most of the time, it does create the potential for a man-in-the-middle attack on your data.

One way to avoid sending username and password data in clear text are to configure digest authentication, which uses a basic encryption method to protect the password. This method does not protect the actual data in the protected directory from being intercepted, however. If you want a truly secure authentication method, you should employ SSL and a proprietary login method using a scripted language and local database connection.

Table 2-11 details the Apache directives that relate to authentication.

Table 2-11. *Apache Directives Related to Authentication*

Directive	Values	Recommended Setting(s)
AuthName	Any string value in quotation marks.	Enter something descriptive that gives the user a clue about what they are accessing; for example, AuthName "Employee portal."
AuthType	Basic: username and password authenticate the user Digest: same as basic authentication, but the password is encrypted	Use Basic because this is the authentication most supported by all major browsers. Digest authentication can be buggy in some browsers.
AuthGroupFile	Specifies the location of the group file	Do not include this directive unless you're configuring access for a large number of users.

(*continued*)

Table 2-11. (*continued*)

Directive	Values	Recommended Setting(s)
AuthUserFile	Specifies the location of the password file for use with Basic authentication (The password file is commonly named .htpasswd.)	I'd recommend sticking with convention on this one. It is a good security practice to store your .htpassword file outside your web-accessible directories to avoid a direct request.
AuthDigestFile	Specifies the location of the password file for use with Digest authentication	Using this directive isn't recommended at this time. Not all browsers support Digest authentication.
User	Specifies that a distinct user or users are allowed to access the protected area	Unless you're keeping a central .htpasswd file and want to further limit access to a protected directory, you don't need this directive.
Require	valid-user, user *username,* group *groupname,* file-owner, file-group	The most used option is required-user since most people choose to maintain separate .htpasswd files.
Satisfy	Any All	By default, Apache chooses the All option. However, if you want users to meet one requirement or another, use the Any option.

Creating a .htpasswd File

Let's say you want to protect `https://apachebook.com/employees/`, allowing only people with a specific username and password to access the URL.

Apache uses a password file to store the users it's allowed to provide access to. As a result, you need to create this file to use Apache's authentication module. This stores passwords using an encryption algorithm in a format that Apache understands.

To create your own password file, you can use the htpasswd tool, which comes bundled with Apache on macOS and Linux. XAMPP on Windows doesn't make this tool available to the command line but does provide a Shell utility that provides the htpasswd tool.

Run the following command to create a new `.htpasswd` file, using *employees* as the username you want people to use for authentication. You should create this file in the directory you want to be protected.

```
htpasswd -c .htpasswd employees
```

You are prompted to enter and confirm a password for the user, and a new file is created in the `employees` directory named `.htpasswd`. The following is what you see in your terminal.

```
swiftly:employees darren$ htpasswd -c .htpasswd darren
New password:
Re-type new password:
Adding password for user darren
swiftly:employees darren$
```

Now that you've got your password file created at `/Users/darren/sites/primary/employees/.htpasswd`, you can configure Apache to protect the directory with basic authentication.

Basic Configuration

Configuring basic authentication is a two-part process. First, you must set up your password file. This file is most often named `.htpasswd`, and should reside in a non-web-accessible area on your web server so that the file isn't accessible to web users. Second, you must configure an `.htaccess` file in the directory you wish to protect.

A standard setup for basic authentication looks like the following.

```
AuthName "Protected Directory. Employees only."
AuthType Basic
AuthUserFile /Users/darren/sites/primary/employees/.htpasswd
Require valid-user
```

When you (or anyone else) attempt to access `https://domain.com/employees/`, the browser pops up a dialog box that asks for a username and password. If you don't supply the right one, you are shown an error message and prevented from accessing the URL's contents.

Adding New File Types

Apache generally knows only a few file extensions as web content: `.html`, `.htm`, `.shtml`, and `.cgi` in general. If it encounters a file extension it doesn't know, Apache treats the file as a plain text document and displays it as such. While this is good most of the time, there are occasions on which you want to use a different file extension. For example, when adding PHP files to your website, you must tell Apache how to handle files with the `.php` file extension.

The installation program for packages such as PHP often handles this, but you should know how to set up new file types in Apache just in case something goes wrong. It's also useful for creating custom file extensions if you want to obscure the programming language used by scripts, for example.

Configuring mime.types

The first step in creating new file types is to add a new entry to the `mime.types` configuration file or add to an existing entry. For example, if you wanted files with a `.content` extension to be treated as HTML files, you would need to search for the `text/html` line, and edit it to match the following.

```
text/html               html htm content
```

Including External Configuration Files

The `include` directive in Apache allows you to maintain several Apache configuration files separately, which are then included as part of the main `httpd.conf`. This is an extremely useful directive, especially in situations in which you're running multiple domains on a single host, or if you want users to have the ability to access and change the configurations for their directories on the server.

Creating multiple configuration files lets you keep the core configuration of the web server safe from prying fingers while letting people change configurations for their own services. It's also an extremely effective way of managing your server's configuration. For example, you could set up several configuration profiles by creating multiple configuration files, which let you adjust Apache's settings depending on the expected load. Alternatively, you could create a "safe" configuration for troubleshooting purposes.

Applying Changes

Once you've made changes to your Apache configuration files, you need to apply them. If you've edited an .htaccess file, there are no further steps for the configuration changes. They are loaded the next time the directory is requested.

However, if you've made changes to the httpd.conf file or files included in the httpd. conf configuration file, you must restart Apache for the changes to take. Thankfully, Apache has included tools so you can do just that. On macOS and Linux, Apache is controlled by a utility called apachectl. To restart the Apache server using the apachectl utility, run the following.

```
apachectl graceful
```

There is also an apachectl restart command; however, if you use graceful to restart your web server, you avoid disconnecting users who are currently on the server. Two other commands are available for controlling the web server: shutdown and start. You should only use these commands if you expect to take the web server down for an extended time for maintenance and if you do not want *any* connections made to it.

The final command is apachectl configtest. I highly recommend using this to test any configuration changes you've made before restarting the server, as it prevents Apache from shutting down due to a typo or invalid configuration.

Note   In Windows, you use the XAMPP control panel to restart Apache.

Summing It Up

You now have Apache installed and configured to its defaults. You're almost ready to go live with your website! You've learned about file types, configuring modules, and updating the default Apache configuration. I also covered rewriting URLs, protecting sites behind a username and password, and creating custom error pages that match your website's look and feel.

In the next chapters, you use the directives you learned in this chapter to set up virtual hosts. You also learn about modules, log files, and scripting languages. And you set up a secure server, all built using the knowledge from this chapter.

CHAPTER 3

Configuring Virtual Hosts

Ah, the wonders of modern technology.

In the early days of the web, it wasn't very common for people to have their own domain names. Hosting was hard to come by, and when you could find it, it was anywhere from $50 to $300 a month, plus up to $75 a year for the domain name itself. I recall one ISP in my hometown was selling a luxury hosting package that included 300 kilobytes of storage and 150 megabytes of traffic for $100 a month. A far cry from the discount hosting of today!

As a result, most websites had impossibly long directory structures to remember to access them directly, but you only needed one server machine to run the web server on. For example, the first website I published was a personal site located at `http://mypage.direct.ca/s/solas/`. Not exactly the most memorable URL. (The evolution of that site now sits at `http://staticred.com`, which I think you will agree is a much more memorable domain.)

Obviously, this has changed in the last few years, and the number of registered domain names has increased dramatically to the point where it's hard to find a domain name that isn't already registered.

As a result of the explosion in domain name ownership, the Apache group needed to add a virtual hosting feature to Apache, which granted the ability for multiple domains to share a server instead of placing each domain on its own server. As far as the domain and the browser are concerned, the domain has its own dedicated server, and the need for long, convoluted paths is removed.

Virtual hosting works by listening to the requests sent to the Apache web server to determine which domain is being accessed, then directing the traffic to the proper directory to find the files requested. In this way, you can completely segregate websites on your server without worrying about things such as file conflicts.

And, as it turns out, this works well for setting up multiple local development sites with their own custom domain names without having to purchase and find hosting!

© Darren James Harkness 2022
D. J. Harkness, *Apache Essentials*, https://doi.org/10.1007/978-1-4842-8324-0_3

A Quick and Dirty Guide to Domains

You've been using domain names as long as you've been on the Internet. But there's a good chance you don't know exactly how they work. This knowledge is useful as I start talking about setting up virtual hosts and development domains. So, let's take a short tour through what domain names are and how they work.

Computers like numbers. The Internet operates primarily on a series of numbers called IP addresses. These are like latitude and longitude for the Internet, providing computers and servers a way of finding each other within an extremely large network.

The early Internet used a system called IPv4, which looks similar to the following.

```
172.16.254.1
```

This provides computers with a network (the first two numbers) and the host (the second two numbers). Each of the four numbers runs from 0 to 255, though some combinations of numbers are reserved for special use. For example, an IP address that starts with 10.0 or 192.168 refers to a local network that is unavailable to the Internet. IP addresses also generally do not use 255 because it is used for broadcasting. By combining these numbers, IPv4 supported over 4 billion unique IP addresses.

As the Internet grew, however, enough devices were connected that this limit was in danger of being exceeded. So IPv6 was created, which provided many more unique addresses (to be precise, 340,282,366,920,938,463,463,374,607,431,768,211,456, or more than 340 *undecillion*, which is an actual word I just had to look up). Although this limit can eventually be hit, the likelihood of running out is extremely low.

An IPv6 address looks something like the following.

```
001:0db8:85a3:0000:0000:8a2e:0370:7334
```

This breaks down similarly to IPv4; the first four numbers refer to the subnet (similar to the network in IPv4), and the second four numbers refer to the interface ID (similar to IPv4's host).

You might notice something with both IPv4 and IPv6: they're not memorable or easy to read. And at this point, you're wondering how this all relates to domain names like Google.com, Facebook.com, or any other website addresses you're used to regularly seeing. This is where DNS (Domain Name System) comes in. It translates a human-readable (and therefore much more memorable) domain name into an IP address behind the scenes.

For example, DNS maps the human-readable google.com to the machine-readable IPv4 address 172.217.14.206.

DNS works from right to left when reading a domain name and breaks it down into three parts. For `www.apachebook.com`, shown in Figure 3-1, the TLD is `.com`, the domain name is **apachebook**, and the subdomain is `www` (a common website subdomain). Many sites don't include the subdomain, using only the domain name and TLD—for example, `apachebook.com`.

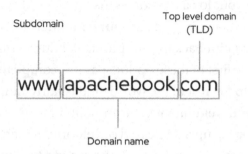

Figure 3-1. *Parts of a domain name*

What Are Virtual Hosts?

One of the benefits of DNS is that there is no strict 1:1 mapping of a domain name to an IP address. Multiple domain names can be assigned to a single IP address, allowing a single server to handle multiple websites. Because each domain name shares a single host, they are referred to as *virtual* hosts. This allows a single Apache instance to handle multiple websites concurrently without having to set up separate servers.

For example, I run `apachebook.com` (the website for this book) on the same server as my personal site, `staticred.com`, a Slack app I created, `today.shipton.io`, and a few others. None of these domains are particularly complex or take up a bunch of bandwidth. Setting these up as virtual hosts on the same Apache installation helps reduce my hosting costs.

I also use virtual hosts in another context: development. I currently have around ten virtual hosts in Apache on my workstation for various projects. Each one has its own domain name set up. For example, `today.local` for the Today app's website, `apache.local` for development on apachebook.com, and `personal.local` for my personal site. These domains are only available from my workstation and work even when I'm not connected to the Internet.

Creating Development Domains

The previous edition of this book took readers through installing and configuring Bind, a tool to manage the translation of domain names to IP addresses over the Internet. For setting up local development domains, this is complete overkill. So, I'm going to simplify it to make your life better.

There are three ways that you can go about this: using the local `hosts` file to configure ad hoc domain names for your local IP address, using a tool like ngrok that sets up temporary domain names that point back to your computer, and creating subdomains via your hosting provider that point back to your public IP address on the Internet.

I recommend using the first of these options, as it is completely self-contained, does not open your computer to the rest of the world, and is fairly simple to set up. However, you may want to make the development environment on your computer available to others, or you might be setting up a dedicated development machine that you want access to regardless of where you are. For that, the second two options are better. Make sure you read up on securing your Apache setup in Chapter 5.

I also recommend that unless you specifically create a subdomain, you set up all of your development domains with the `.local` TLD. This special-use TLD is reserved for this purpose to avoid issues with pre-existing domain names.

Using the hosts File to Manage Local Domains

macOS, Windows, and Linux all have an easy method of specifying ad hoc local domain names that don't require you to register the domain or set up complicated DNS software. Each of these operating systems contains a file called `hosts`, which acts as a local reference for DNS lookups and overrides.

You can find the `hosts` file at `/etc/hosts` on macOS and Linux. On Windows, you can find it at `c:\windows\system32\drivers\etc\hosts`. On all operating systems, this file is protected, and you need to use administrative privileges to save your changes to the file.

Once you have found the `hosts` file, edit it with administrative privileges to create a local development domain that points to the IP address for localhost (always 127.0.0.1). When you open this file for editing, you see some examples already exist. But in general, the format is as follows.

```
domainname        ip.address
```

Here's an example of what an entry looks like.

```
apachebook.local        127.0.0.1
```

Because domain names are just easy-to-remember references for IP addresses, you can associate multiple domains against a single IP address. And this is where things get useful for local development because you can set up something like the following.

```
client-a-site.local       127.0.0.1
client-b-site.local       127.0.0.1
client-c-site.local       127.0.0.1
my-playground.local       127.0.0.1
```

That's four different local domains that point to the exact same Apache installation, but separate working directories on your computer.

```
/Users/darren/code/client-a/
/Users/darren/code/client-b/web/
/Users/darren/code/client-c/public/
/Users/darren/code/playground/
```

You can also use the `hosts` file to point local domain names to a different IP address. For example, I use a Raspberry Pi for my personal dashboard. On my workstation, I've added this to my `hosts` file.

```
dashpi.local       192.1681.1.42
```

If you are using an old desktop or a Raspberry Pi for a development environment, you can use the preceding example to set up your local domains.

I'll get into how to configure Apache for this shortly.

Using ngrok to Manage Local Domains

If you don't feel comfortable editing system files (an admirable trait), don't fret. There are tools available that manage local domains for you, such as ngrok (`https://ngrok.com`) and localtunnel (`https://localtunnel.github.io/www/`). These tools create a tunnel between your computer and its server through which Internet traffic can travel. They're a relatively safe way to create domain names that are accessible through the Internet, regardless of where you are.

Let's run through a setup using localtunnel, a free service offered under an open source license.

First, you need to install localtunnel. There's a quick start tutorial available at `http://localtunnel.me` that uses npm to install it globally. Once installed, the `lt` command is available in your terminal. You can use this to create a subdomain on the fly to point to your localhost and a port. By passing the `--subdomain` argument, you can also request a specific subdomain that's more memorable.

Here's an example that requests the `apachebook` subdomain, pointing to a Node.js application running locally on port 3000.

```
$ lt --port 3000 --subdomain apachebook
your url is: https://apachebook.loca.lt
```

This domain keeps running as long as the `lt` command runs on your system.

Setting up a Subdomain Pointing to Your Local Environment

Another option, if you manage your domain names and have access to edit DNS records, is to set up a subdomain that branches off your main domain. For example, you might set up a development environment for `https://apachebook.com` called `https://dev.apachebook.com`, with `dev` as the subdomain and `apachebook.com` as the domain.

A simple method for doing this is to use a service like Cloudflare, which provides the ability to quickly set up domains and subdomains separately from your hosting environments. Cloudflare has extensive documentation on how to set this up, which I won't reproduce here. You need to know that you are creating a subdomain to point to your external, public IP address.

Note   You need to configure your router to allow external traffic to reach your internal computer. This varies by Internet provider, so you want to reach out to their support team for help with this.

Why Develop Locally?

Chapter 1 discussed the tiered set of environments most web development organizations use, highlighting the local development environment as a sandbox for the developer to test code as they write it. And this book, so far, has been focused on helping you set up that environment.

A local development environment provides two major benefits.

- It's an always-available environment to test your code, regardless of whether you are connected to the Internet.

- It speeds up testing and debugging while you're developing your codebase.

Local development doesn't require access to the Internet to test your code's functionality. So long as you have Apache configured to load your local virtual domain, you can load a site up in your browser and use it just as you would on the live website.

The ability to quickly test and debug your codebase is the real power of setting up a local development environment, however. Changes can be tested as soon as you save the file, instead of waiting while you upload changes to a remote environment. This might be only a few seconds or so each time. However, that starts to add up quickly as you dig into particularly messy bugs.

Configuring Apache's Virtual Hosts

You can configure virtual hosts directly within the `httpd.conf` file or you can create separate files for each virtual host, then import them into the `httpd.conf` via that Import directive. To maintain central control over your Apache configuration, place the virtual host configurations within your `httpd.conf`. However, if you want users on your system to have the ability to change their own Apache configurations, or you want to make domain maintenance more efficient, you should create separate files for each domain. For example, `apachebook.com.conf` would be created for the `apachebook.com` domain, whereas `staticred.com.conf` would be created for the `staticred.com` domain.

The only difference between the configuration for a virtual host and that for a regular domain is the `<VirtualHost>` directive and its supporting directives: `ServerName` and `ServerAlias`. The actual configuration of a virtual host is identical to setting up your main domain.

A Sample Apache Configuration

Here's a sample configuration for a virtual host in Apache.

```
<VirtualHost 127.0.0.1>
    ServerAdmin darren@staticred.com
    DocumentRoot /Users/darren/code/apachebook.local
    ServerName apache.local
    ServerAlias www.apache.local
    ErrorLog /Users/darren/code/apachebook.local/error.log
    CustomLog /Users/darren/code/apachebook.local/access.log combined
    <Directory /Users/darren/code/apachebook.local >
        Options Indexes Includes FollowSymLinks MultiViews
        AllowOverride All
    </Directory>
   ScriptAlias /cgi-bin/ /Users/darren/code/apachebook.local/cgi-bin/
    <Directory /Users/darren/code/apachebook.local/cgi-bin>
        Options Indexes Includes FollowSymLinks MultiViews ExecCGI
        AllowOverride All
    </Directory>
</VirtualHost>
```

The important directives to note here are the following.

- `VirtualHost`
- `ServerAdmin`
- `DocumentRoot`
- `ServerName`
- `ServerAlias`
- `ErrorLog`
- `CustomLog`
- `ScriptAlias`
- `<Directory>`

Let's break each one of those down.

<VirtualHost>

The `<VirtualHost>` directive tells Apache that the configuration within it refers to a secondary domain on the server rather than the primary domain. It takes two parameters: the IP address of the domain and the port. The syntax is as follows.

```
<VirtualHost 11.22.33.44:port>
```

Often, this is the only IP address available on the server. Occasionally, however, a single server may have more than one IP address, so you need to specify which IP address to use. An example is in the Apache documentation, where the server is to be made available on both the Intranet (where it has an IP address of 192.168.1.2) and the Internet (where it has an IP address of 204.255.176.199). The `<VirtualHost>` directive would look like the following.

```
<VirtualHost 192.168.0.2 204.255.176.199>
```

Although the IP address isn't required in the configuration, it's a very good idea to include it. This saves Apache some time in recognizing the domain name, as it won't have to ask the DNS server to look it up.

As I mentioned, you can specify the port if you are not running Apache on the standard port (80). The directive to configure Apache to use port 8080 is as follows.

```
<VirtualHost 204.255.176.199:8080>
```

You can also include the following above the `<VirtualHost>` directive to perform the same function.

```
Listen 204.255.176.199:8080
```

ServerAdmin

This is identical to the `ServerAdmin` directive used in the primary domain's configuration. However, in the context of virtual hosting, the `ServerAdmin` directive should be changed to point to the email address of the person looking after the domain. This way, any troubles with the domain are emailed directly to them.

The syntax of the `ServerAdmin` directive is as follows.

```
ServerAdmin user@host.com
```

DocumentRoot

The `DocumentRoot` directive works exactly as it does in the primary domain's configuration but points to the public html directory of your domain's primary user instead of the primary domain's main directory. In the case of staticred.net, this would point to `/var/home/staticred.net/public_html/`. It is a good idea to separate the document root directories for different domains to avoid confusion. Mimicking the user hierarchy is a good way of managing things.

In Windows, it's a good idea to create a `c:\htdocs` folder and place each subdomain within it. For example, the staticred.net domain would be in `c:\htdocs\staticred.net\`, and the staticred.com domain would be in `c:\htdocs\staticred.com\`. By default, XAMPP installs the `htdocs` directory within its directory in the Program Files folder. Moving this to the root makes it easier to find your files in Explorer.

The syntax is as follows.

```
DocumentRoot </path/to/directory>
```

ServerName and ServerAlias

Here's where the actual domain configuration comes in. The `ServerName` directive takes a single parameter: the domain name. It looks something like the following.

```
ServerName staticred.net
```

After you've declared the primary domain name for the virtual host, you can now set up aliases for it. The most common one, of course, is www. You could also set up `ww.staticred.net` or `wwww.staticred.net` (common mistyped subdomains). You could even go wild and set up `a.little.bit.of.staticred.net`.

`ServerAlias` is also useful to point completely different domain names to the same `DocumentRoot` without having to duplicate configurations. For example, you could register two domains—`domaina.com` and `domainz.com`—and set up `domaina.com` in the `ServerName` directive and `domainz.com` in the `ServerAlias` directive. No matter which of the domains a browser requested, the same content would be sent back. This is the secret trick of the bulk domain registry sites to park thousands of domains on their servers.

The syntax of the `ServerAlias` directive is as follows.

```
ServerAlias <subdomain.domain.com>
```

ErrorLog and CustomLog

The ErrorLog and CustomLog directives set up individual log files for each domain. I'd highly recommend this practice, as it makes things such as statistical analysis and archiving much easier in the long run. The ErrorLog directive stores Apache runtime information and messages from your scripting environment; the CustomLog stores the activity between Apache and its web clients.

The syntax for the ErrorLog and CustomLog directives is as follows.

```
ErrorLog /path/to/error.log
CustomLog /path/to/access.log type
```

The ErrorLog directive is relatively straightforward: you need only point it to the location of the domain's error.log file. The CustomLog directive takes an additional parameter, which tells which type of access log to record. More information can be found in Chapter 6.

ScriptAlias

The ScriptAlias directive in the virtual host configuration is identical to that in the main domain configuration. However, you want to point the ScriptAlias to a unique directory for every domain. This way, you can keep CGI scripts separate from one domain to another and avoid scripts from one domain conflicting with another domain's scripts.

The first parameter of the ScriptAlias directive sets up the name of the CGI directory, as Apache sees it, and is relative to the DocumentRoot. The second parameter points to the physical location of the scripts directory.

One of the most useful reasons for using the ScriptAlias directive is to be able to use CGI scripts that live outside of your DocumentRoot directory. For example, you have two domains whose DocumentRoot directives point to different folders. However, you want to share CGI scripts between the two of them. Using the ScriptAlias directive, you can place the CGI scripts within DocumentRoot for the first domain, then point the second domain's ScriptAlias to that folder; it appears the folder exists on both domains.

The syntax for the ScriptAlias directive is as follows.

```
ScriptAlias /cgi-bin/ /home/staticred/public_html/cgi-bin/
```

Directory

After configuring the main document root directory for Apache, you need to specify options for it by creating a `<Directory>` entry. This sets the actual configuration of your website within Apache and controls what access files on your website have.

```
<Directory /var/www/>
    Options Indexes Includes FollowSymLinks MultiViews
    AllowOverride All
    Order allow,deny
    Allow from all
</Directory>
```

This can be broken down pretty easily. In the `<Directory>` directive, you need to specify the directory you're configuring. Since you want to configure the main domain, you should match the `DocumentRoot` directory, `/var/www`. If you want to specify options for a different directory, say `/cgi-bin`, you would add another section, like the following.

```
<Directory /var/www/cgi-bin>
    Options Indexes Includes FollowSymLinks ExecCGI MultiViews
    AllowOverride All
</Directory>
```

This section would allow CGI files to be executed in the `/cgi-bin` directory, but not within the rest of your website. This allows you to contain all script files in a single directory, making it easier to audit what scripts are running on your Apache server.

When you configure a directory, you also configure all its subdirectories. So, when you make changes to `/var/www`, the changes would also be applied to `/var/www/images`. To give special configurations to individual subdirectories within your main `DocumentRoot`, you must create separate `<Directory>` entries for each. After you tell Apache which directory you want to set options for, you need to tell it which options to configure the directory with. Table 3-1 lists the many options that you can set on a directory.

Table 3-1. *Available Options in Apache*

Option	Description	Should I use it?
All	Enables all options except MultiViews. This is the default setting.	If you're looking for a quick way to configure a directory and are not concerned about performance or security, then yes. Otherwise, specify your options manually.
ExecCGI	Allows CGI files to be executed in the directory (generally using the Perl programming language). This should only be enabled for directories containing scripts because enabling it for all directories causes Apache to take a hit on its performance.	You should use this only for directories that contain CGI files. Note that you do not need to use this setting for PHP files within a directory.
FollowSymLinks	If this Is enabled, the server follows symbolic links within a directory. Symbolic links are similar to Windows shortcuts; they point to other files or directories within a UNIX system. This option is ignored if used within a <Location> directive.	Yes. It allows you to set up shortcuts to files and directories without duplicating documents on your system. This is a side benefit because you only need to edit the original file, and all symbolic links are automatically updated.
Includes	If server-side includes (SSI) are enabled on your Apache server, this option allows HTML files to use all functions of SSI, including the #exec function.	No. Most modern websites no longer use SSI, as languages such as PHP offer this functionality. If you are using SSI, it's recommended to use the IncludesNOEXEC option.

(continued)

Table 3-1. (*continued*)

Option	Description	Should I use it?
IncludesNOEXEC	This option is identical to the Includes option but doesn't enable the #exec function. The #exec function allows an HTML document to execute a system command.	Yes, if you are using SSI. This option is identical to the Includes option but removes the #exec function from SSI.
Indexes	If no documents matching the ones specified in the DocumentIndex directive are found (index.html, for example), Apache returns a formatted directory listing of the requested URL.	This option can be enabled or disabled, depending on the level of security that you want on your Apache server. If this option is enabled, it shows users a listing of the files within a directory. Though this is fine for most applications, you may not want it for others (for example, a directory that contains script files). If this option isn't enabled, a request for a directory that doesn't contain a DocumentIndex file returns a 403 forbidden error.
MultiViews	The MultiViews directive searches for files matching the requested file. For example, Apache displays the closest match if a requested file doesn't exist on the server.	This is recommended so that you can catch any mild typos made by people requesting URLs.
SymLinksIfOwnersMatch	IT is identical to the FollowSymLinks option but only follows the symbolic link if it's owned by the same user on the system as the original directory. If the same user does not own the symlink, the symbolic link is not followed.	It's a good idea to enable this option if you want to preserve security within your system. For example, if you allow users on your system to have their own websites through user directories, enabling this option is a good idea.

Using Separate Configuration Files

A great way to maintain your virtual hosts is to separate them into individual configuration files. You can quickly find and make changes to a domain's directives using individual configuration files. You can also give control of the domain configuration to individual users on the system without compromising the other domains or the main Apache configuration. As far as Apache is concerned, it's as though you included the information into the main httpd.conf.

To import files into the `httpd.conf`, you can use the `Include` directive, which takes the following syntax.

```
Include /path/to/file.conf
```

If you set up two configuration files for local domains, `personal.local` and `company.local`, you would put the following in `httpd.conf`.

```
Include /usr/local/etc/extra/http-personal.conf
Include /usr/local/etc/extra/http-company.conf
```

The best practice with the Include directive is to specify the file's absolute physical path. However, you can also specify paths relative to the Apache `ServerRoot` directory. The same file (assuming `ServerRoot` were set to `/etc/apache`) would be as follows.

```
Include extra/file.conf
```

Once you have separated the configuration into individual files, you can give read/write permissions to allow users to modify their domain information.

Putting It All to Work

Now you have everything you need to set up multiple development instances using Apache. Let's run through an example where you create a development environment for a personal portfolio dev site and a client dev site for Cree Incorporated.

Pointing the Virtual Domains to Your Local Computer

First, let's add the virtual domains to our hosts file. Add the following lines.

```
127.0.0.1     personal.local
127.0.0.1     creeinc.local
```

Save the file, and test it out by opening your terminal and pinging the virtual domains. Here's an example for personal.local (the -c4 option stops after four pings. If you don't add this, you can stop pinging the domain by pressing Ctrl+C).

```
$ ping -c4 personal.local
PING personal.local (127.0.0.1): 56 data bytes
64 bytes from 127.0.0.1: icmp_seq=0 ttl=64 time=0.033 ms
64 bytes from 127.0.0.1: icmp_seq=1 ttl=64 time=0.240 ms
64 bytes from 127.0.0.1: icmp_seq=2 ttl=64 time=0.131 ms
64 bytes from 127.0.0.1: icmp_seq=3 ttl=64 time=0.100 ms

--- personal.local ping statistics ---
4 packets transmitted, 4 packets received, 0.0% packet loss
round-trip min/avg/max/stddev = 0.033/0.126/0.240/0.075 ms
```

You should see something similar to this. If not, check your /etc/hosts file to ensure it's using the right values.

If you are using a dedicated device like a Raspberry Pi for your dev server, then you need to use its internal IP address instead of 127.0.0.1 in your hosts file.

Configuring Apache for Multiple Virtual Hosts

Once you've set up the virtual domain on your computer, it's time to start configuring Apache. Open your terminal and head to the configuration directory specified for your operating system in Table 1-6 in Chapter 1.

On Windows and macOS, you find a sample virtual hosts configuration file in the extra directory called httpd-vhosts.conf. This file contains all your virtual host configurations.

On Linux, the configuration file needs to be created in the sites-enabled directory. You can create a single file for all configurations, like Windows and macOS, or you can create individual files for each site. For simplicity, I recommend following the Windows and macOS models. Create a new file called 000-vhosts.conf.

In your virtual hosts configuration file, add the following. Change the location of the DocumentRoot and `<Directory>` to match your own public web document locations (see the "Where to Put Your Website Files" section in Chapter 1).

Note   The following examples assume a code repository where support files are in the main directory and publicly accessible web documents are in a subdirectory named `public`.

```
<VirtualHost *:80>

    # Sets the document directory to our personal site.
    DocumentRoot "/Users/darren/code/personal-site/public"

    # Tells Apache what domain to listen for requests to
    ServerName personal.local

    # Configure logging for the virtual domain. This separates
    # out each domain into its own log files for easier scanning.
    ErrorLog ${APACHE_LOG_DIR}/personal.local-error.log
    CustomLog ${APACHE_LOG_DIR}/personal.local-access.log combined

</VirtualHost>

<Directory /Users/darren/code/personal-site/public>
    # Allow .htaccess files to be used
    AllowOverride All

    # Configures index.html or index.htm to be the
    # default page for each directory. For PHP-based
    # sites, this configuration will be
    # DirectoryIndex index.php index.html
    DirectoryIndex index.html index.htm

    # Turn on symbolic link following and multiviews
    Options FollowSymLinks Multiviews

    # Configures Multiviews to match any file.
    MultiviewsMatch Any
```

```
    # Lets anyone access the virtual domain
    Require all granted
</Directory>

<VirtualHost *:80>

    # Sets the document directory to our personal site.
    DocumentRoot "/Users/darren/code/creeinc/public"

    # Tells Apache what domain to listen for requests to
    ServerName creeinc.local

    # Configure logging for the virtual domain. This separates
    # out each domain into its own log files for easier scanning.
    ErrorLog ${APACHE_LOG_DIR}/creeinc.local-error.log
    CustomLog ${APACHE_LOG_DIR}/creeinc.local-access.log combined

</VirtualHost>

<Directory /Users/darren/code/creeinc/public>
    # Allow .htaccess files to be used
    AllowOverride All

    # Configures index.html or index.htm to be the
    # default page for each directory. For PHP-based
    # sites, this configuration will be
    # DirectoryIndex index.php index.html
    DirectoryIndex index.html index.htm

    # Turn on symbolic link following and multiviews
    Options FollowSymLinks Multiviews

    # Configures Multiviews to match any file.
    MultiviewsMatch Any

    # Lets anyone access the virtual domain
    Require all granted
</Directory>
```

Finally, open your main Apache configuration, `httpd.conf` (or `apache.conf`) and load the configuration file(s) you have just created through the `Include` directive.

Here's an example on macOS.

```
# Virtual hosts
Include /usr/local/etc/httpd/extra/httpd-vhosts.conf
```

Save this file, and then restart your Apache web server. When Apache has restarted, you can test your local environments in your browser. Figure 3-2 is an example of what comes up for the first virtual host configured at `http://personal.local`.

Figure 3-2. *Your local virtual host (well, mine actually)*

Summing It Up

In this chapter, you learned about configuring Apache for virtual hosts. You used the hosts file to manage local domains through custom DNS settings, using a tool such as ngrok to create tunnels for local development or setting up a custom subdomain to point back to your local development environment. With that in place, you also learned how to configure Apache to support multiple local development domains through its VirtualHost functionality, which allows you to host multiple domains through a single Apache installation.

Now that you understand how to set up multiple development environments in your Apache installation, let's move on to the next step: configuring Apache to support scripting languages like PHP and Node.js. I'll see you there.

CHAPTER 4

Scripting Languages

At some point in your life as a professional working on the Web, you're going to have to work with scripting languages. I know it's a pain in the butt, but I resisted it as long as possible. But I eventually gave in, and so will you (cue dramatic music).

It's really not as bad as it seems. I started on my journey toward scripting languages with server-side includes (SSI), a feature of Apache that lets you break HTML documents down into components that could be included by the server, similar to how modern templating systems like Twig or Smarty work. I'd been developing websites the old-old fashioned way, by editing individual HTML documents and uploading them to the web server. It was brutal, grueling work that caused me hours of grief whenever any changes needed to be made to the look and feel of a website. SSI allowed me to configure specific header and footer files and place them in a central location; this freed up my content from the presentation and made global look/feel updates quick and painless since I was now only editing a single global document.

As PHP grew in popularity and templating systems started gaining traction, the world moved on from SSI, which is no longer commonly used. Where SSI allowed me to separate my content from its presentation, PHP gave me the freedom to separate my content from its source. Scripting languages like PHP allow you to generate content dynamically, retrieve information from and store it on a database, accept and process user information, and even tell you when there's something wrong with the website itself.

In this book, I focus on configuring Apache for two scripting languages: PHP and server-side JavaScript using the Node.js framework.

JavaScript has rapidly grown as a server-side language through the Node.js and React frameworks. Although it's the language of choice for a fraction of sites compared to PHP, it's being used by some notable folks, including Twitter, Spotify, *The New York Times*,

© Darren James Harkness 2022
D. J. Harkness, *Apache Essentials*, https://doi.org/10.1007/978-1-4842-8324-0_4

and the *Daily Mail*.[1] Many boot camps and web-development schools now prioritize teaching their students JavaScript over PHP.

Apache has also added support for several programming languages, such as Python, Ruby, C# (through the Mono framework), Lua, Perl, R, and TCL. But, as these aren't as frequently used, I'll leave it to other authors to give you a hand setting them up.

PHP

PHP has been around for a long time and is now a robust language. As of this writing, 78% of websites are built using a form of PHP, including Facebook, Instagram, Wikipedia, and Slack.[2] Because it has been around for so long, it has gained a solid reputation among web developers as a reliable, stable, and fast language. It's well established as a scripting language for the Web and will most likely be the language you encounter, especially if you are working with a CMS such as WordPress, Drupal, or Craft CMS.

Installing PHP

If you're using XAMPP on Windows, congratulations, you're done! You can move on to this chapter's "Configuring PHP" section. XAMPP installs PHP alongside Apache and takes care of the configuration for you. It might still be useful to read through this section, however, if you want to make changes to PHP's settings.

For the rest of you, I'm to walk through installing and configuring PHP on Apache, as it's not included in a basic Apache installation. But no fear! It's not hard!

Installing PHP on macOS

Apple used to include a default installation of PHP as a part of macOS. Unfortunately, as of macOS 12.0 Monterey, this is no longer the case. So, first things first. You need to get PHP installed! Like installing Apache, let's use Homebrew to get PHP on our system.

Open your terminal application and type the following.

```
brew install php
```

---

[1] https://w3techs.com/technologies/details/pl-js
[2] https://w3techs.com/technologies/details/pl-php

This installs the most recent stable version of PHP on your system. As of this writing, that's PHP 8.0.12. If you need an older PHP version for your projects, you can specify this as part of the install command with the @ modifier. For example, WordPress and Craft CMS both require PHP 7.4 and are not fully stable on PHP 8 (as of the writing of this book).

To install PHP 7.4, your command would be the following.

```
brew install php@7.4
```

Like the install, this throws a bunch of text onto your screen. That's OK. we're just concerned with the end bit in the Caveats section, paying attention to the full path for the php7_module. and the path for the PHP configuration files (usually in /usr/local/etc/php/). Homebrew also reminds you of what needs to be configured in Apache. But don't worry. I cover that in the "Configuring PHP" section of this chapter. Jot these down in your notebook, however. You'll need these paths later.

```
==> Caveats
To enable PHP in Apache add the following to httpd.conf and restart Apache:
    LoadModule php7_module /usr/local/opt/php@7.4/lib/httpd/modules/
    libphp7.so

    <FilesMatch \.php$>
        SetHandler application/x-httpd-php
    </FilesMatch>

Finally, check DirectoryIndex includes index.php
    DirectoryIndex index.php index.html

The php.ini and php-fpm.ini file can be found in:
    /usr/local/etc/php/7.4/

php@7.4 is keg-only, which means it was not symlinked into /usr/local,
because this is an alternate version of another formula.

If you need to have php@7.4 first in your PATH, run:
    echo 'export PATH="/usr/local/opt/php@7.4/bin:$PATH"' >> ~/.profile
    echo 'export PATH="/usr/local/opt/php@7.4/sbin:$PATH"' >> ~/.profile
```

```
For compilers to find php@7.4 you may need to set:
  export LDFLAGS="-L/usr/local/opt/php@7.4/lib"
  export CPPFLAGS="-I/usr/local/opt/php@7.4/include"

To restart php@7.4 after an upgrade:
  brew services restart php@7.4
Or, if you don't want/need a background service you can just run:
  /usr/local/opt/php@7.4/sbin/php-fpm --nodaemonize
==> Summary
   /usr/local/Cellar/php@7.4/7.4.27: 498 files, 72.3MB
```

Installing PHP on Linux

Installing PHP for Apache on Linux is a pleasure if you use a distribution with package management, such as Ubuntu. To install the latest stable PHP and a default configuration for Apache, simply open a terminal and type the following.

```
sudo apt-get install libapache2-mod-php
```

This installs PHP and configures it for Apache, including editing the Apache configuration files for you to point to the correct location. At the end of the installation process, you are given the location of PHP's configuration files. Jot these down in your notebook, so you can refer to them later (generally, they are stored in /etc/php by version number; for example, /etc/php/7.4/). Jot this directory down in your notepad. You'll use this later. It's worth noting that there are *two* configuration files to keep track of—one for the terminal (CLI) and another for Apache.

Configuring Apache for PHP

Now that you have PHP installed, you need to configure Apache to properly handle requests that need PHP to function. If you are using XAMPP on Windows, you can skip this section, as PHP is already configured in Apache.

On macOS and Linux, Apache is not automatically configured to support PHP, even when installing both. You need to configure Apache yourself using the following guides.

On macOS

Like other scripting languages, Apache supports PHP through an Apache module. In your `httpd.conf`, look for the "Dynamic Shared Object (DSO) Support" section. This is the section Apache uses to load libraries for additional functionality.

At the end of this section, add the following line, replacing 7.4 with the version you have installed (e.g., `php@8.1` for PHP 8.1). The path for this module file is what you jotted down from Brew's Caveats section in the previous installation step.

```
LoadModule php7_module /usr/local/opt/php@7.4/lib/httpd/modules/libphp7.so
```

Note   As of PHP 8, the module name no longer refers to the version of PHP installed. For the preceding, replace `php7_module` with `php_module` and `libphp7.so` with `libphp.so`.

That load the PHP module when Apache starts up. However, you still need to configure Apache to understand when to invoke the PHP module. First, you need to add `index.php` as a valid index file that Apache should load when requesting a directory. Search for the `DirectoryIndex` directive and replace it with the following.

```
DirectoryIndex index.php index.html
```

This instructs Apache to first look for a file named `index.php` when a directory is requested, and if no `index.php` file is found, to next look for `index.html` as a fallback. If neither file is found, Apache returns an error or shows a directory listing if the `<Directory>` section sets `Indexes` as an `Option` (see Chapter 2 for more information on this).

Next, you need to configure Apache's handling of PHP files. In general, PHP files use the `.php` file extension. However, some alternatives are used alongside it, as listed in Table 4-1.

Table 4-1. *File Extension Alternatives*

Extension	Description
.phar	PHP Archive. It allows a PHP application and its supporting files (such as CSS and images) to be bundled as a single archive file.
.phtml	Used when there is little or no data logic. These files tend to focus on presentation instead of providing functionality. It's a very old file extension used in PHP 2.x and not very common in modern applications.
.phps	PHP Source files. These are not functional PHP files and are intended to only display the included PHP source code as HTML.

This configuration can be added by creating a new file in the extra directory called `httpd-php.conf`. Put the following in this file.

```
<FilesMatch ".+\.ph(ar|p|tml)$">
    SetHandler application/x-httpd-php
</FilesMatch>
<FilesMatch ".+\.phps$">
    SetHandler application/x-httpd-php-source
    # Deny access to raw php sources by default
    # To re-enable it's recommended to enable access to the files
    # only in specific virtual host or directory
    Require all denied
</FilesMatch>
# Deny access to files without filename (e.g. '.php')
<FilesMatch "^\.ph(ar|p|ps|tml)$">
    Require all denied
</FilesMatch>
```

This is a bit more than what's recommended after installing PHP using Homebrew but offers a bit more security and stability. The first section of this configuration configures Apache to invoke the PHP module for any files that use the following extensions.

- .phar
- .php
- .phtml

The second section prevents Apache from rendering files with the `.phps` file extension. Files with this extension contain PHP code but are intended to be displayed as plain text. This isn't recommended, so I suggest keeping this section in.

Finally, the last section denies access to a set of dot files (files with an extension but no filename). Generally, you should deny access to such files because they could contain secure or sensitive information.

- `.phar`
- `.php`
- `.phps`
- `.phtml`

Once you have saved the `httpd-php.conf` file, you need to go back to your `httpd.conf` and let Apache know to include its contents as part of its configuration. At the bottom of `httpd.conf`, enter the following (replacing `php7_module` with `php_module` for PHP 8.x installations).

```
<IfModule php7_module>
Include /usr/local/etc/httpd/extra/httpd-php.conf
</IfModule>
```

This instructs Apache to load the file's contents as part of its configuration.

Once all this is complete, you can check the config using the following.

```
apachectl configtest
```

Then restart Apache through the following command.

```
brew services restart httpd
```

On Linux

The PHP install script you ran on Ubuntu creates two configuration files in `/etc/apache2/mods-available`: `php7.4.load` and `php7.4.conf`. For Apache to include these files in its configuration, you must ensure they are set up in `/etc/apache2/mods-enabled/`. This can be accomplished by either copying the files or creating a symbolic link (the preferred method).

To create a symbolic link, open your terminal and navigate to /etc/apache2/mods-enabled. Enter the following commands.

```
sudo ln -s /etc/apache2/mods-available/php7.4.load php7.4.load
sudo ln -s /etc/apache2/mods-available/php7.4.conf php7.4.conf
```

Configuring PHP

Now that you have PHP installed and set up within Apache, you should take some time to update the standard configuration. This includes making configuration changes for things such as upload file size and memory usage and enabling some extensions that will be useful for later development.

Updating Default Configuration

By default, the configuration for PHP is pretty decent. You don't *have* to make any changes to start developing locally, but I recommend making the following changes to provide a more flexible development environment.

Note   Whenever you change the configuration values or add new directives in your `php.ini` configuration file, you need to restart Apache for the changes to take effect.

Increasing the Memory Usage Limit

When using a development environment, you don't need to be as concerned about memory usage as you would be in a staging or production environment. PHP is configured by default to use 128 MB of memory for any script's execution.

If you are working with code that heavily uses data or complex data models, you may want to increase the amount of memory used to help debug your code.

You can do this through the `memory_limit` configuration directive by specifying a different memory limit.[3] To make things easier, you can append a size modifier to the end of the number, using M for megabytes and G for gigabytes.

```
memory_limit = 512M
```

This sets the memory limit for each script execution to 512 MB. If you wanted to increase this to a full gigabyte of memory, you'd instead use the following.

```
memory_limit = 1G
```

This will, to no surprise, increase the amount of memory available to a script to 1 GB. I wouldn't recommend going this high, as this can cause problems when moving to production. You should instead try reducing the amount of memory your script takes up. I recommend starting with 128 MB and increasing if you see memory errors in your error logs.

Increasing the Upload File Size

The default upload limit in PHP is 2 MB, which often doesn't work well for projects such as content management systems. As such, you want to increase the maximum allowed file size for uploading by editing the `upload_max_filesize` directive.[4]

Like the `memory_limit` directive, you can use a size modifier appended to the number, using M for megabytes and G for gigabytes. Most importantly, you don't need a huge file size limit set. However, you may work with PDFs or other documents that take up space. I'd suggest setting this to 200 MB, using the following.

```
upload_max_filesize = 200M
```

You can, of course, edit this as you see fit.

Configuring Noisy Error Reporting

Production servers are generally configured to disable or heavily minimize error reporting so that log files do not grow too large. But this also means that valuable troubleshooting data is lost.

---

[3]`www.php.net/manual/en/ini.core.php#ini.memory-limit`
[4]`www.php.net/manual/en/ini.core.php#ini.upload-max-filesize`

Since you're setting up a development environment, you want as much error reporting as possible. This creates "noisy" error logs, which means more information is available to help debug our programming problems.

First, you need to ensure that error reporting is turned on. Open your php.ini and search for the following: `display_errors`.[5] This directive controls whether errors are reported to the page when viewing a script in the browser. By default, this is set to On, but it is often changed to Off for production so that errors are not displayed to the end user, which might create confusion.

Let's ensure that the directive is configured like the following.

```
display_errors = On
```

Next, let's configure PHP's level of logging when encountering problems. This is configured through the `error_reporting` directive.[6]

If you have installed PHP 8, you can safely ignore this section. PHP 7, however, is configured to record all errors *except* notices, coding standards warnings, or code that will be deprecated in future versions of PHP. This is great for production, where you only want to report when something fatal happens.

On your development server, however, you want as much information as possible, since it may be useful for troubleshooting later. Search for the `error_reporting` directive (it should be near the display_errors directive) and modify it to match the following.

```
error_reporting = E_ALL
```

This configures PHP to report any warnings, errors, and notices it encounters when attempting to execute a script.

Increasing Max Execution Time

Most servers running websites are purpose-built for that role. The resources available are dedicated to Apache, and whatever scripting languages are used. Often, even database services are set up on separate servers.

If you're setting up Apache on your laptop or desktop, that is not the case. Apache, databases, and scripting languages will all compete for resources alongside your editing

---

[5]www.php.net/manual/en/errorfunc.configuration.php#ini.display-errors

[6]www.php.net/manual/en/errorfunc.configuration.php#ini.error-reporting

environment, communications tools, and browsers, which means that scripts take a little longer to run than they would on a dedicated or virtual server.

If you find that your PHP scripts are failing with a timeout error, then you need to adjust your timeout through the `max_execution_time` directive. This directive defines how long PHP waits, in seconds, until stopping the execution of the script. By default, this is set to 30 seconds, which is fine for most operations. However, if you are working with a lot of data or a lot of operations at once or are pulling data from an external source, you may want to increase this amount. Open the `php.ini` used by Apache, and search for the `max_execution_time` directive.

Here's an example that sets the timeout to 60 seconds.

```
max_execution_time = 60
```

Installing PHP Extensions

Note   For Windows users who have installed XAMPP, installing PHP extensions that are not included with XAMPP is a bit of a tricky affair. Best to put this book down for a moment and hit up your favorite search engine if you need to install a non-standard PHP extension.

Like Apache, PHP adds functionality through a module-based system. In PHP, these are known as extensions. There are extensions available for caching, connecting to databases, manipulating graphics files, and parsing data.

I'd recommend installing the following commonly used extensions.

- cURL

- GD Graphics Library

- MySQLi (or MariaDB)

- PDO::MySQL

To install an extension, open php.ini and search for the "Dynamic Extensions" section. Here, you see a list of extensions commented out with a semi-colon, such as `;extension=curl`.

Find the extension you wish to enable and remove the semi-colon. For the recommended modules, ensure the following is included in the "Dynamic Extensions" section.

```
extension=curl
extension=gd2
extension=mysqli
extension=pdo_mysql
```

Your projects might require additional extensions to be enabled, such as `gettext` or `intl`. For example, Craft CMS requires the following PHP extensions to be enabled to support its functions that are not enabled by default.

- cURL

- GD Graphics Library

- JSON (included in PHP 8, but a separate extension in earlier versions of PHP 7)

- MBString

- PDO::MySQL

Recommended php.ini

The following is an example of `php.ini`'s contents. Several additional PHP directives can be included in this file, but the following should be configured as part of any PHP installation. I included a description of what each directive does, along with recommended values.

Note   Any time you make changes to your PHP configuration, you need to restart Apache.

```
; Turns on PHP's scripting engine
engine = On

; Enables or disables PHP short tags. These are not generally
; recommended, as they may create issues with other file formats,
```

```
; such as XML.
short_open_tag = Off

; Configures how much output data, in bytes, is buffered before being
; sent in response to to a browser's request. 4096 bytes is recommended
output_buffering = 4096

; Configures which PHP functions are disabled. This is useful for
; Apache-based installs, where you do not want to open access to
; powerful and potentially damaging functions.
disable_functions = pcntl_alarm,pcntl_fork,pcntl_waitpid,pcntl_wait,pcntl_
wifexited,pcntl_wifstopped,pcntl_wifsignaled,pcntl_wifcontinued,pcntl_
wexitstatus,pcntl_wtermsig,pcntl_wstopsig,pcntl_signal,pcntl_signal_get_
handler,pcntl_signal_dispatch,pcntl_get_last_error,pcntl_strerror,pcntl_
sigprocmask,pcntl_sigwaitinfo,pcntl_sigtimedwait,pcntl_exec,pcntl_
getpriority,pcntl_setpriority,pcntl_async_signals,pcntl_unshare,

;;;;;;;;;;;;;;;;;;;
; Resource Limits ;
;;;;;;;;;;;;;;;;;;;

; Configures the amount of time, in seconds, PHP waits on a script
; before failing and reporting an error. Default is 30 seconds. For
; development environments, it may be useful to increase this to 60
; seconds.
max_execution_time = 60

; Configures the amount of memory available to a running PHP script.
; By default, this is 128 megabytes, but should be increase for data-
; heavy applications.
memory_limit = 128M

;;;;;;;;;;;;;;;;;;;;;;;;;;;;;;;;;;;
; Error handling and logging ;
;;;;;;;;;;;;;;;;;;;;;;;;;;;;;;;;;;;

; Configures which errors PHP reports. Production usually ignores
; deprecation errors, compatibility notes, and notices. For a
; development environment, we want to report everything.
```

```
error_reporting = E_ALL

; Enables or disables errors being returned as part of its output. By
; default this is disabled, reporting errors only to the log files. For
; development environments, it is often useful to display these errors
; within the browser.
display_errors = On

; Enables or disables logging of errors to Apache.
log_errors = On

;;;;;;;;;;;;;;;;;;
; Data Handling ;
;;;;;;;;;;;;;;;;;;

; Determines which super global arrays are registered when PHP starts.
; The below registers $_GET, $_POST, $COOKIE, and $SERVER
variables_order = "GPCS"

; Determines the order data is registered into the $_REQUEST super
; variable. This places GET first, and PUT second
request_order = "GP"

; Enables or disables the $argc and $argv variables. These are mostly
; used when a PHP script is used from the command line. Since Apache
; doesn't work this way, I recommend disabling them to increase
; performance.
register_argc_argv = Off

; Enables or disables Just In Time processing for the $_REQUEST and
; $_SERVER variables. This means they aren't created until they're
; used in the script, increasing performance.
auto_globals_jit = On

; Configure the maximum size of POST data. The default is 8 megabytes,
; which is generally considered sufficient.
post_max_size = 8M

; Configures the default MIME type sent to the browser, which helps it
; to render the content. In general, we want to keep the default value.
```

```
default_mimetype = "text/html"

; Configures the character set sent to the browser, which helps it to
; render individual characters correctly. This is important when making
; use of non-alphanumeric extended characters.
default_charset = "UTF-8"

;;;;;;;;;;;;;;;;;
; File Uploads ;
;;;;;;;;;;;;;;;;;

; Enables or disables the ability to receive files uploaded via
; a user's browser.
file_uploads = On

; Configures the maximum allowable file size for uploads. We will
; configure this for 200 megabytes.
upload_max_filesize = 200M

; Configures how many files can be uploaded from a user's browser
; simultaneously.
max_file_uploads = 20

;;;;;;;;;;;;;;;;;;;;;
; Fopen wrappers ;
;;;;;;;;;;;;;;;;;;;;;

; Configures the ability to use URLs in PHP's fopen() function. This is
; useful for loading external data files like JSON or CSV.
allow_url_fopen = On

; Configures the ability to use external URLs in PHP's include()
; function. Since this function is most commonly used for including
; PHP functionality, it's not recommended to allow this.
allow_url_include = Off

; Configures the default timeout, in seconds, when connecting to an
; external URL. This could be increased to support connecting to slow
; APIs.
default_socket_timeout = 60
```

93

```
;;;;;;;;;;;;;;;;;;;;;;;
; Dynamic Extensions ;
;;;;;;;;;;;;;;;;;;;;;;;

; Enables the cURL extension
extension=curl

; Enables MySQLi
extension=mysqli

; Enables the GD2 graphics library
extension=gd2

; Enables the PDO extension for MySQL, which provides additional
; functionality for secure data handling
extension=pdo_mysql

;;;;;;;;;;;;;;;;;;;;;
; Configure MySQLi ;
;;;;;;;;;;;;;;;;;;;;;

[MySQLi]

; Configure the number of persistent links. We'll set this to -1, which
; indicates no limit
mysqli.max_persistent = -1

; Enables or disables persistent connections to a MySQL server.
mysqli.allow_persistent = On

; Configures the number or links allowed to a MySQL server. We'll set
; this to -1, which indicates no limits
mysqli.max_links = -1

; Configures the default port for connecting to a MySQL server.
; Generally, this is port 3306
mysqli.default_port = 3306

; Enable or disable reconnecting to the MySQL Server. This is disabled
; by default, and I recommend leaving this setting.
mysqli.reconnect = Off
```

```
;;;;;;;;;;;;;;;;;;;;;;;
; Configure Sessions ;
;;;;;;;;;;;;;;;;;;;;;;;

[Session]

; Configures how PHP stores and retrieves session data. This saves the
; data securely as files, which helps manage memory usage.
session.save_handler = files

; Enables or disables strict session mode. This is a security option,
; disabled by default, which requires a session ID be created before
; working with session data.
session.use_strict_mode = 0

; Enables or disables the use of Cookies within PHP
session.use_cookies = 1

; Enables or disables the use of a cookie for storing and maintaining
; the session ID. This is highly recommended for security.
session.use_only_cookies = 1

; Configures the name of the session stored in the cookie. This is
; configured to use the contents of a PHP constant.
session.name = PHPSESSID

; Configures the serializer used by PHP for session data.
session.serialize_handler = php

; Configures the expiry of data for session data, in seconds, before it
; is automatically removed.
session.gc_maxlifetime = 1440
```

Testing It Out

After making changes to your php.ini to support your particular codebase, restart Apache and navigate to your DocumentRoot. Create a file named index.php and include the following PHP script.

```php
<?php
phpinfo();
```

This simple script calls the phpinfo() function, which returns information about your PHP installation. Save the file, and open this URL in your browser: http://localhost/index.php. You see a screen similar to Figure 4-1.

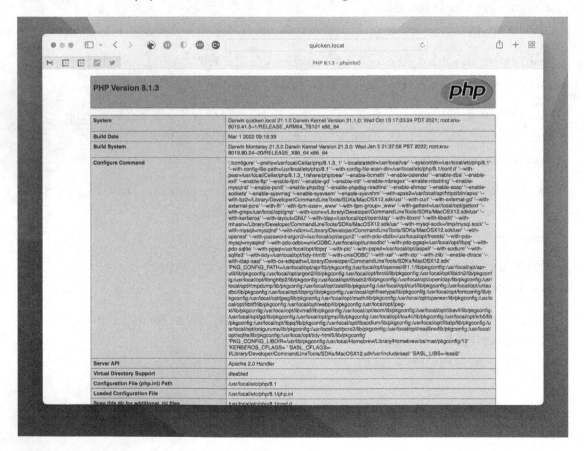

Figure 4-1. *PHP configuration page*

This contains a wealth of information about your PHP configuration, including its version, installed extensions, and the Apache `DocumentRoot`. It's extremely useful as a troubleshooting tool in development environments.

Configuring Node.js on Apache

When I wrote the first edition of this book in 2004, PHP was an up-and-coming scripting language that was beginning to eat into the dominance of Perl, which was the more prevalent language for building dynamic, functional websites at the time. Writing this chapter in 2022, I feel a bit of deja vu as I discuss Node.js and PHP. PHP is still, by far, the more prevalent scripting language for building web applications and websites, but Node.js is starting to eat away at that.

Node.js applications operate differently from PHP-based ones; where PHP-based sites require a web server such as Apache or nginx to handle the traffic, Node.js applications are built to be self-sufficient applications in their own right, managing network traffic and requests internally. When setting up a Node.js application for production, they're often set up as system services so that the Node.js application restarts when the system is hosted on reboots.

The standard model for running Node.js applications on a development environment is to use Express and set up a transitory server through a command in your terminal, such as the following.

```
node app.js
```

This starts up a server built into the node application, which listens for connections on a specified port, such as 3000, waiting for users to access the application.

And, for the most part, this is fine for development. However, you might want something running a bit more permanently, where you don't have to keep a terminal window up and running, ensuring that the node application isn't interrupted. You might also want to run multiple Node.js applications without memorizing what port each is running on.

This is where Apache can become very useful. You can combine Apache's virtual hosts with its ability to act as a reverse proxy or gateway server.

Configuring Your Node.js Application for Apache

Node applications are not, by their nature, persistent. Each Node application runs as its own runtime executable, separate from the server it is deployed to. On the one hand, this is extremely convenient, as you do not necessarily need to configure a full web server to deploy your Node application. However, it also means that your Node application is *only* accessible so long as that runtime is active. You must manually restart it if it's interrupted for any reason, including a reboot.

Installing pm2

To be always available, you need to run the Node application as a service. There are a couple of options to do this, but the simplest is to use PM2, a process manager for Node. js applications that allows you to easily turn them into services.

To install PM2, open your terminal and type the following.

```
npm install pm2@latest -g
```

Note   You may need to run this as sudo on Linux

This installs PM2 globally.

Configuring the Application

Let's set up a basic Node.js Hello World application to show how things work. Create a new directory in your code directory, and create a new app.js file with the following contents.

```
const express = require('express')
const app = express()

app.get('/', function (req, res) {
  res.send('Hello World!')
})

app.listen(3000, function () {
  console.log('Example app listening on port 3000!')
})
```

Next, you need to create a `package.json` with the following.

```json
{
  "name": "helloworld",
  "version": "0.0.0",
  "description": "",
  "main": "app.js",
  "scripts": {
    "test": "echo \"Error: no test specified\" && exit 1"
  },
  "author": "You!",
  "license": "ISC",
  "dependencies": {
    "express": "^4.15.3"
  }
}
```

This very simple program listens for a connection on port 3000 and outputs "Hello world!" in response. You're not going to win any awards, but it'll do for our example.

You can test to make certain that things are working by typing **node app.js**, then visiting `http://localhost:3000/` in your browser.

Adding Your Application as a Service

Once you've configured your application, you can use PM2 to add it as a service. Type the following into your terminal. After changing to the directory, your Node.js application is stored in (substituting `app.js` with your application's main entry point).

```
pm2 start app.js
```

You see something similar to the following.

```
[PM2] Spawning PM2 daemon with pm2_home=/home/darren/.pm2
[PM2] PM2 Successfully daemonized
[PM2] Starting /var/www/sites/nodejs/helloworld/app.js in fork_mode
      (1 instance)
[PM2] Done.
```

id	name	mode	↻	status	cpu	memory
0	app	fork	0	online	0%	29.3mb

Configuring Apache's Reverse Proxy

Here's where the magic comes in. By combining what you've learned about virtual hosts with a feature in Apache that lets you configure it as a gateway for other services, you can create an always-up development service that allows for memorable domain names instead of remembering a set of cryptic port numbers for your Node.js applications.

The full documentation for Apache's reverse proxy is at `https://httpd.apache.org/docs/2.4/howto/reverse_proxy.html` if you are interested in learning more. However, you should only need what's on the following pages for this use.

Enabling Apache's Proxy Modules

Apache's reverse proxy functionality is handled through two modules: `mod_proxy` and `mod_http`. These need to be enabled in your Apache installation to set up a persistent Node.js site.

On macOS and Windows

Open your `httpd.conf`, and look for the following line (the paths to `mod_proxy.so` and `mod_proxy_http.so` differ on macOS and Windows).

```
#LoadModule proxy_module lib/httpd/modules/mod_proxy.so
```

Uncomment this directive by removing the #, so that you have the following.

```
// On Mac OS:
LoadModule proxy_module lib/httpd/modules/mod_proxy.so
LoadModule proxy_http_module lib/httpd/modules/mod_proxy_http.so
```

```
// On Windows using XAMPP:
LoadModule proxy_module modules/mod_proxy.so
LoadModule proxy_http_module modules/mod_proxy_http.so
```

Test your configuration and restart Apache for the changes to take effect.

On Linux

Open a terminal and navigate to /etc/apache2/mods-enabled.
Type the following.

```
ln -s ../mods-available/proxy.load proxy.load
ln -s ../mods-available/proxy_http.load proxy_http.load
```

This adds in a call to the LoadModule directive for the mod_proxy.so and mod_proxy_http modules in Apache. You'll configure these later in your virtual host configuration.

Test your configuration and restart Apache for the changes to take effect.

Creating a Virtual Host Configuration

Despite running things through a proxy, you still need to configure Apache to provide a virtual host for the Node.js server. The following configuration creates a domain in Apache for http://nodeapp.local, and configures it to pass requests through a configured proxy to port 3000 (instead of port 80, the default port for most URLs).

```
<VirtualHost *:80>
    DocumentRoot "/var/www/sites/nodeapp"
    ServerName nodeapp.local

    # Set up Logging
    ErrorLog ${APACHE_LOG_DIR}/nodeapp-error.log
    CustomLog ${APACHE_LOG_DIR}/nodeapp-access.log combined

    <IfModule mod_proxy.c>
        ProxyPass / http://portly.local:3000
        ProxyPassReverse / http://portly.local:3000/

        <Proxy *>
            Order allow,deny
```

```
          Allow from all
      </Proxy>
    </IfModule>
</VirtualHost>
```

Testing It Out

Once you have the preceding configured, visit `http://nodeapp.local` in your browser, and you should see something similar to Figure 4-2.

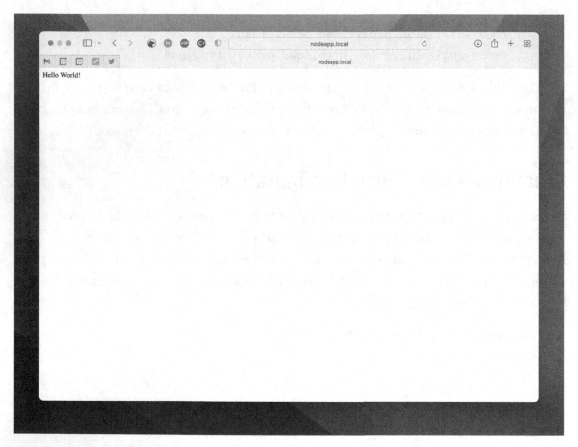

Figure 4-2. *Loading your local Node.js development environment*

If your Node.js app is not running, you see something like Figure 4-3.

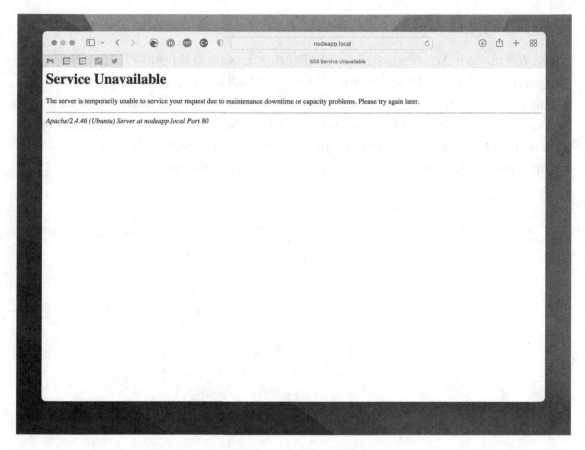

Figure 4-3. *Apache's error page when loading a non-running Node.js application*

Configuring React Apps on Apache

If you're building a React application and want to use Apache's virtual hosts to allow for simplified domain names, you have two options.

First, follow the directions for Node.js applications, and configure Apache as a reverse proxy that accesses the Node Express server included in your React application.

Alternatively, you can configure Apache to point `DocumentRoot` to your React application's public folder. If you follow this path, ensure that Apache is configured to use gzip compression. To do so, you want to enable the `mod_deflate` module in Apache.

Summing It Up

Phew! You made it. You learned about configuring Apache to support PHP and Node.js in this chapter. For PHP, you now know how to install and configure PHP and then configure Apache to support it. Node.js was a little trickier, but you learned how to support a persistent virtual domain that connects to the Node.js server through a proxy.

The next chapter discusses one of the most important aspects of Apache's configuration: setting it up for secure communications on the web.

## CHAPTER 5

Securing Your Setup

You use the secure web every day without even thinking about it. With privacy laws, trillions of dollars, euros, and yen, and corporate communications have grown exponentially over the past 20 years. It was important to find a way for information on the Internet to be transmitted securely. Browsers do this through HTTPS (HyperText Transfer Protocol Secure). Whenever you see a small lock beside the website's name in your browser, you're accessing it through HTTPS.

HTTPS uses a technology called Secure Socket Layers (SSL) that encrypts traffic between a web server and a web browser.

SSL at a Glance

SSL is used for much more than just serving websites securely. It protects confidential email and secure FTP sessions over the Internet and can be applied to other Internet communications. It's basically an extremely complicated, prime number-driven form of pig Latin.

Netscape developed SSL in 1994 to solve a distinct problem. People discovered that the web wasn't nearly as secure as they'd hoped. They had already started to want to use the Internet for something other than mindless entertainment and email joke lists. They wanted to start using it to sell merchandise, create employee-only sites, and conduct financial transactions. It was clear that standard HTTP wouldn't cut it since all the data traveled on plain text. They needed a secure way to transfer information between the browser and the server.

Several people came up with solutions for the problem; since Netscape had the lion's share of the browser market, their solution won. Netscape wanted to make SSL as seamless as possible for the user, beyond giving them a notice that they were about to enter a secure connection, the user shouldn't have to do anything.

© Darren James Harkness 2022
D. J. Harkness, *Apache Essentials*, https://doi.org/10.1007/978-1-4842-8324-0_5

They achieved that goal: people use SSL daily without thinking about it. Unfortunately, if you want to configure Apache to support secure socket layers, you *do* have to think about it. So, let's move on.

Configuring SSL for Subdomains

Configuring SSL for subdomains is much easier now than when this book's first edition was written. Two tools are now available that greatly simplify the process: LetsEncrypt and Certbot.

When the first edition of *Apache Essentials* was written, obtaining a secure certificate that worked with SSL was difficult and expensive. LetsEncrypt.org was created in 2012 to make it easier to set up secure websites, removing both financial and technical barriers to adoption. Certbot is a companion utility that automates registering and renewing SSL certificates from LetsEncrypt.

This section explains using these tools to create a signed certificate for your subdomain.

Installing Certbot

First, you need to install the Certbot application on your system. This tool registers and renews certificates from LetsEncrypt and installs them in Apache for you.

On macOS

Let's use Homebrew to install Certbot. Open your terminal and type the following.

```
brew install certbot
```

This downloads the latest version of Certbot and installs it on your system.

On Linux

On Linux, you need to install Certbot with your package manager. Open a terminal and type the following.

```
sudo apt-get install certbot
```

On Windows

On Windows, you need to download the installer and install it on your system. You can find the current Windows installer at https://certbot.eff.org.

Running Certbot

Once Certbot is installed, you can run it to generate a certificate for your subdomains.

If you've already set up Apache for your local subdomains, you can run Certbot with the Apache plugin. Open a terminal and type the following.

```
sudo certbot certonly —apache
```

This reads your Apache configuration files and lets you select which configuration to generate a certificate for.

Here's an example for the subdomain local.apachebook.com.

```
sudo certbot certonly —apache

Saving debug log to /var/log/letsencrypt/letsencrypt.log
Plugins selected: Authenticator apache, Installer apache

Which names would you like to activate HTTPS for?
- - - - - - - - - - - - - - - - - - - - - - - - - - - - - - - - - - - - - - - - -- - - -
1: local.apachebook.com
2: errors.local
3: nodeapp.local
- - - - - - - - - - - - - - - - - - - - - - - - - - - - - - - - - - - - - - - - - - - - -
Select the appropriate numbers separated by commas and/or spaces, or
leave input
blank to select all options shown (Enter 'c' to cancel): 1
Cert not yet due for renewal
You have an existing certificate that has exactly the same domains or
certificate name you requested and isn't close to expiry.
(ref: /etc/letsencrypt/renewal/local.apachebook.com.conf)
```

```
What would you like to do?
- - - - - - - - - - - - - - - - - - - - - - - - - - - - - - - - - - - - -
1: Keep the existing certificate for now
2: Renew & replace the certificate (may be subject to CA rate limits)
- - - - - - - - - - - - - - - - - - - - - - - - - - - - - - - - -- - - - -
Select the appropriate number [1-2] then [enter] (press 'c' to cancel): 2
Renewing an existing certificate for local.apachebook.com
IMPORTANT NOTES:
 - Congratulations! Your certificate and chain have been saved at:
   /etc/letsencrypt/live/local.apachebook.com/fullchain.pem
   Your key file has been saved at:
   /etc/letsencrypt/live/local.apachebook.com/privkey.pem
   Your certificate will expire on 2022-08-13. To obtain a new or
   tweaked version of this certificate in the future, simply run
   certbot again. To non-interactively renew *all* of your
   certificates, run "certbot renew"
 - If you like Certbot, please consider supporting our work by:
   Donating to ISRG / Let's Encrypt:   https://letsencrypt.org/donate
   Donating to EFF:                     https://eff.org/donate-le
```

Pay attention to those important notes at the end of Certbot's output. It contains the full paths for the certificates it's created (or renewed). Jot these paths down because you'll use them later in this chapter.

Now that Certbot has run and installed the new certificates, you can configure Apache by jumping to the "Configuring Apache for HTTPS" section later in this chapter. The certificate you created is stored in the location indicated in Table 5-1, depending on your operating system. Write it down so you can reference it in that section.

***Table 5-1.** Location of Certificate Files Downloaded by Certbot*

Operating System	Location
macOS	/opt/etc/letsencrypt/live/subdomain.domain.tld/
Linux	/etc/letsencrypt/live/subdomain.domain.tld/
Windows	C:\Certbot\live\subdomain.domain.tld\

Configuring HTTPS for Local Domains

Unfortunately, Certbot and LetsEncrypt aren't available to use for localhost or domains ending in the `.local` TLD. For this, let's dig into things in much more detail.

Setting up a Local SSL Certificate Authority

As I mentioned earlier, every certificate must have a certificate authority to verify its authenticity. If the authenticity of a certificate can't be verified, then the browser won't trust the connection. When you set up a local development environment and want to use SSL, you must set up your own certificate authority (CA).

Note   Most browsers notify end users that the certificate they use does not come from a known CA. For your first visit to a local development environment, you must instruct your browser to trust and install the certificate.

Installing OpenSSL

Local SSL certificates are managed through an application called OpenSSL. You must install the OpenSSL application on your operating system to create and manage local certificates.

macOS

On macOS, you use Homebrew to install OpenSSL. Open a terminal and type the following.

```
brew install openssl
```

Linux

On Ubuntu, OpenSSL is available via its package manager. Open a terminal and type the following.

```
sudo apt-get install openssl
```

Windows

If you're using XAMPP, you're done! XAMPP comes preinstalled with a server certificate, and no additional configuration is required. OpenSSL is installed, however, and available at `C:\xampp\apache\bin\openssl.exe`.

Storing Your Certificates

First, you must have a secure place to store your CA certificates and key files.

You find them in `/usr/local/etc/openssl` on macOS.

You find them in `/etc/ssl` on Linux.

You find them stored in `c:\xampp\apache\conf\ssl.crt\` and `C:\xampp\apache\conf\ssl.key\` on Windows.

For UNIX and macOS X systems, your best place to store these is in the `/etc/ssl` directory. For Windows, store them in the `C:\OpenSSL\ca\` folder.

1. Create the certificate authority directory. In Linux, this should be stored in /etc/ssl/ca/private; in Windows, I'd suggest storing it in `C:\OpenSSL\ca\private`. Create the CA private keys directory.

    ```
    mkdir -p /etc/ssl/ca/private
    ```

2. Then, set the permissions of the certificate authority directory to be readable by root or administrator only. Nobody but the root user or administrator should have access to the directory that your root certificates are in. If other people can access the root certificates, they can use them to decode the encrypted data between the server and a browser. For Linux or macOS X, type the following at the command prompt.

    ```
    chown -R root /etc/ssl/ca/
    ```

Generating the CA Private Key

Now that they have a place to go, you can create the key files for the CA. To do so, you must use the OpenSSL utility, supplied with the OpenSSL libraries. To start this tool, change to the directory you just created and type **openssl**.

```
dev:/etc/ssl# openssl
```

Note   Windows users need to specify the full path to the OpenSSL utility, which is at C:\xampp\apache\bin\openssl.exe.

After you start the OpenSSL utility, you are presented with an OpenSSL> prompt. Now, you can start entering commands to create your CA files. The first file you need to create is the actual key file. This file contains a random string that creates your encrypted data. There are several different encryption types. RSA is the most popular because it is the most supported encryption among browser makers.

To generate an RSA key, run the genrsa command. It takes three parameters: -des3, which selects TripleDES as the encryption format; -out, which specifies the filename to write the RSA key to; and finally, a bit-length for the encrypted key. The recommended bit-length is 2048. As part of the process, you are asked for a password for the private key. Enter a unique, hard-to-guess password for your CA private key. Anyone who gains access to this password can create new certificates using this key, allowing them to successfully identify themselves as your server.

```
OpenSSL> genrsa –des3 -out ca.key 2048
```

When you run the command, the utility displays a bunch of information on the screen.

```
warning, not much extra random data, consider using the -rand option
Generating RSA private key, 1024 bit long modulus
.......................++++++
....++++++
e is 65537 (0x10001)
Enter PEM pass phrase:
Verifying password - Enter PEM pass phrase:
OpenSSL>
```

Next, you must request a new certificate from the CA through the req command. This uses the CA's private key and some distinct information about your installation to create a unique public certificate. This command creates the public key you distribute to your website users and creates new server certificates.

Creating a Public CA Certificate

The public CA certificate creates and/or signs new server certificates. This is also the file that is distributed to users of your server to authenticate that the server key is correct.

To create the public CA certificate, you must use OpenSSL utility's req command. The req command takes three parameters: -new tells OpenSSL to create a new key; -key tells it which CA key to base it on, and -out specifies the file to which the certificate is written.

```
OpenSSL> req -new -x509 -days 365 -key ca.key -out ca.crt
```

When run, the req command asks for some information about your installation. The following is an example of the type of information it asks for and sample responses. You can leave fields blank if you wish, but the more information you supply with the certificate, the more confidence the end users have that it is secure.

```
Using configuration from /usr/lib/ssl/openssl.cnf
You are about to be asked to enter information that will be incorporated
into your certificate request.
What you are about to enter is what is called a Distinguished Name or a DN.
There are quite a few fields but you can leave some blank
For some fields there will be a default value,
If you enter '.', the field will be left blank.
-----
Country Name (2 letter code) [AU]:CA
State or Province Name (full name) [Some-State]:British Columbia
Locality Name (eg, city) []:Port Coquitlam
Organization Name (eg, company) [Internet Widgits Pty Ltd]:Apache
Essentials
Organizational Unit Name (eg, section) []:
Common Name (eg, YOUR name) []:localhost
Email Address []:hello@apachebook.com
OpenSSL>
```

A new key, ca.csr, is written to the directory, and you are returned to the OpenSSL> prompt. Before you can use this new public key, you must sign it. The x509 command does this. The following command makes a new certificate (ca.crt) that expires after one year (365 days). After it expires, you must generate a new CA public key. The following shows the syntax of the x509 command and its output.

```
OpenSSL> x509 -req -days 365 -in ca.csr -signkey ca.key -out ca.crt
Signature ok
subject=/C=CA/ST=Alberta/L=Edmonton/O=Apache Essentials/OU=Admin/CN=Darren
James Harkness/Email=hello@apachebook.com
Getting Private key
OpenSSL>
```

Signing Your Own Certificates

In most OpenSSL distributions, a script named sign.sh is included. This script signs new certificates from the CA. There are a couple of things you need to make sure of before running the sign.sh script.

1. Ensure that you have created a server private key and a certificate request file (server.csr).

2. Copy the server.csr file to the CA private directory (/etc/ssl/ca/private).

Once you've got everything in the right place, you can run the sign.sh script, and tell it which file to sign. It looks something like the following.

```
./sign.sh server.csr
```

Here's a sample of the sign.sh script output.

```
CA signing: server.csr -> server.crt.
Using configuration from ca.config
Check that the request matches the signature
Signature ok
The Subjects Distinguished Name is as follows
countryName           :PRINTABLE:'CA'
stateOrProvinceName   :PRINTABLE:'British Columbia'
localityName          :PRINTABLE:'Port Coquitlam'
organizationName      :PRINTABLE:'Apache Essentials'
commonName            :PRINTABLE:'http://apache.local'
emailAddress          :IA5STRING:'hello@apachebook.com'
```

```
Certificate is to be certified until May  1 00:49:36 2023 GMT (365 days)
Sign the certificate? [y/n]:y
1 out of 1 certificate requests certified, commit? [y/n]y
Write out database with 1 new entries
Data Base Updated
CA verifying: server.crt <-> CA cert
server.crt: OK
```

When the server.crt file has been written, you can move it and the original server.key file to /etc/apache/ssl. Ensure that the server.key file is made readable only to root or the administrator. Review the "Creating a Public CA Certificate" section for more information on how to do this.

The sign.sh Script

If you don't have a sign.sh script, you can create it using the following code.

```
#!/bin/sh
##
##   sign.sh -- Sign a SSL Certificate Request (CSR)
##   Copyright (c) 1998-2001 Ralf S. Engelschall, All Rights Reserved.
##

#   argument line handling
CSR=$1
if [ $# -ne 1 ]; then
    echo "Usage: sign.sign <whatever>.csr"; exit 1
fi
if [ ! -f $CSR ]; then
    echo "CSR not found: $CSR"; exit 1
fi
case $CSR in
   *.csr ) CERT="`echo $CSR | sed -e 's/\.csr/.crt/'`" ;;
       * ) CERT="$CSR.crt" ;;
esac

#   make sure environment exists
if [ ! -d ca.db.certs ]; then
```

```
    mkdir ca.db.certs
fi
if [ ! -f ca.db.serial ]; then
    echo '01' >ca.db.serial
fi
if [ ! -f ca.db.index ]; then
    cp /dev/null ca.db.index
fi

#   create an own SSLeay config
cat >ca.config <<EOT
[ ca ]
default_ca              = CA_own
[ CA_own ]
dir                     = .
certs                   = \$dir
new_certs_dir           = \$dir/ca.db.certs
database                = \$dir/ca.db.index
serial                  = \$dir/ca.db.serial
RANDFILE                = \$dir/ca.db.rand
certificate             = \$dir/ca.crt
private_key             = \$dir/ca.key
default_days            = 365
default_crl_days        = 30
default_md              = md5
preserve                = no
policy                  = policy_anything
[ policy_anything ]
countryName             = optional
stateOrProvinceName     = optional
localityName            = optional
organizationName        = optional
organizationalUnitName  = optional
commonName              = supplied
emailAddress            = optional
EOT
```

```
# sign the certificate
echo "CA signing: $CSR -> $CERT:"
openssl ca -config ca.config -out $CERT -infiles $CSR
echo "CA verifying: $CERT <-> CA cert"
openssl verify -CAfile ca.crt $CERT

# cleanup after SSLeay
rm -f ca.config
rm -f ca.db.serial.old
rm -f ca.db.index.old

# die gracefully
exit 0
```

Configuring Apache for HTTPS

Now that you have generated SSL keys and certificates for your subdomain, you can configure Apache to use them. There are a few steps to this.

1. First, you must load the SSL module.

2. Next, you need to configure the global SSL options.

3. Finally, you need to configure the specific server options.

The next sections walk you through the final steps to getting an SSL server up and running.

Creating a Separate Configuration File

I'd suggest creating a separate configuration file for your SSL settings and naming it ssl.conf. This file contains your SSL server's directives and <Directory> statements. By keeping this file separate, you can easily make changes to it, without scrolling through your main httpd.conf to find the relevant sections.

Loading the SSL Module

Obviously, before using SSL, you need to ensure that the mod_ssl module is loaded. This is done through two lines in ssl.conf.

```
LoadModule ssl_module /usr/lib/apache/1.3/mod_ssl.so
AddModule mod_ssl.c
```

Mac users find the module located at lib/httpd/modules/mod_ssl.so. Windows users find it at modules/ssl/mod_ssl.so.

The LoadModule directive tells the Apache server the module's name and where it can find the files for it. Consult Table 5-2 to find the location on your operating system.

Table 5-2. *Location of Apache Modules*

Operating System	Location
Linux	/usr/lib/apache/modules/
macOS	/usr/local/lib/httpd/modules
Windows	C:\xampp\apache\lib

Once the module is loaded, you need to add the module to the server. Use the AddModule directive to do so. Here is an example of adding the SSL module to httpd. conf for Linux.

```
# Depends: setenvif mime socache_shmcb
LoadModule ssl_module /usr/lib/apache2/modules/mod_ssl.so
```

Note   The SSL module also requires that the setenvif, mime, and socache_shmcb modules be enabled in Apache.

Configuring the Apache's SSL Module

Once you've loaded the module, you can start configuring it for use in Apache.

Configuring the Global Options

First, you must set up some default directives for the Apache server.

The first directive is SSLMutex. This directive configures the SSL lock file, which stores session data used by Apache with regard to its operations. You can leave this unconfigured if you're not using session data with your SSL server.

There are three ways to configure this directive, but only one that is useful for UNIX, Windows, and macOS users: sem. This uses a common lock file format that works across all operating systems.

```
SSLMutex sem
```

If, for some reason, sem doesn't work on your system, you can specify a location for the lock file by using the file option. This would look something like the following.

```
SSLMutex file:/var/log/apache/ssl_mutex
```

Next, you need to start the random seed generator through the SSLRandomSeed directive; this, combined with the certificate, ensures that the key to encrypt a session isn't generated using a predictable number. Two parameters are passed to the SSLRandomSeed directive: the method to generate random numbers and the context where the random number generator is accessed.

There are several different methods available with the SSLRandomSeed directive, but only two that you use: builtin and file. The builtin method uses Apache's internal pseudo-random number generator. The upside is that it doesn't take any additional processor power away from your server. The downside is that it isn't as secure as other methods. Windows users want to use this method since no random device exists on a Windows server.

The file: method is available to UNIX servers, but not Windows users, and uses the /dev/random or /dev/urandom devices. These devices are included with most UNIX servers and exist solely to generate random data. Since they are part of the operating system, neither of these devices takes extra processor time to run. If you add a number after the file: method, this limits the amount of data returned from the random device.

Two contexts are available for the SSLRandomSeed directive: startup and connect. The startup context starts the random generator when Apache starts; the connect context starts it when an SSL connection is initiated.

More than one SSLRandomSeed directive can be configured—and it's recommended.

```
SSLRandomSeed startup builtin
SSLRandomSeed startup file:/dev/urandom 1024
SSLRandomSeed connect file:/dev/urandom 1024
```

Next, you need to tell Apache how to deal with its session cache. By default, SSL already handles its own session cache. However, if you're running an extremely busy site, you may notice some performance issues with the default session cache. The `mod_ssl` documentation says that the `SSLSessionCache` directive is useful when parallel requests are made; that is, when requests for a page and the graphics within it are made. The default value for this is

```
SSLSessionCache none
```

If your server is experiencing performance issues, you may want to enable the SSLSessionCache option. There are two options you can use: `dbm` and `shm`. The `dbm` option is recommended in the mod_ssl documentation and promises a noticeable speed increase. The `shm` option gives an even higher performance increase, as it stores the session data to a configured amount of RAM instead of to disk. However, it's not supported by every operating system, so you may be unable to use it.

If you decide to enable `SSLSessionCache`, use the following syntax.

```
SSLSessionCache dbm:/var/log/apache/ssl_cache
SSLSessionCache shm:/var/log/apache/ssl_cach(256000)
```

Finally, you need to tell Apache where to save its log data for secure connections. This is identical to the `ErrorLog` configuration discussed in another chapter.

```
SSLLog /var/logs/apache/ssl.log
SSLLogLevel info
```

The next chapter talks about configuring custom access logs. When the `mod_ssl` module is installed on your server, you can extend custom access logs to SSL. The following log records the time, remote host, SSL protocol, the HTTP protocol and file requested, and finally, the amount of data transferred.

```
CustomLog logs/ssl_request "%t %h %{SSL_PROTOCOL}x %{SSL_CIPHER}x
\"%r\" %b"
```

The `mod_ssl` module adds the ability to use a set of preconfigured server variables outlined in Table 5-3 (`www.modssl.org/docs/2.8/ssl_reference.html#table4`).

Table 5-3. SSL Server Variables

Variable	Type	Description
HTTPS	flag	HTTPS is being used
SSL_PROTOCOL	String	The SSL protocol version
SSL_SESSION_ID	string	The hex-encoded SSL session ID
SSL_CIPHER	string	The cipher specification name
SSL_CIPHER_EXPORT	string	true if cipher is an export cipher
SSL_CIPHER_USEKEYSIZE	number	Number of cipher bits (actually used)
SSL_CIPHER_ALGKEYSIZE	number	Number of cipher bits (possible)
SSL_VERSION_INTERFACE	string	The mod_ssl program version
SSL_VERSION_LIBRARY	string	The OpenSSL program version
SSL_CLIENT_M_VERSION	string	The version of the client certificate
SSL_CLIENT_M_SERIAL	string	The serial of the client certificate
SSL_CLIENT_S_DN	string	Subject DN in client's certificate
SSL_CLIENT_S_DN_x509	string	Component of client's Subject DN
SSL_CLIENT_I_DN	string	Issuer DN of client's certificate
SSL_CLIENT_I_DN_x509	string	Component of client's Issuer DN
SSL_CLIENT_V_START	string	Validity of client's certificate (start time)
SSL_CLIENT_V_END	string	Validity of client's certificate (end time)
SSL_CLIENT_A_SIG	string	Algorithm for the signature of client's certificate

SSL_CLIENT_A_KEY	string	Algorithm for the public key of client's certificate
SSL_CLIENT_CERT	string	PEM-encoded client certificate
SSL_CLIENT_CERT_CHAINn	string	PEM-encoded certificates in the client certificate chain
SSL_CLIENT_VERIFY	string	NONE, SUCCESS, GENEROUS or FAILED:reason
SSL_SERVER_M_VERSION	string	The version of the server certificate
SSL_SERVER_M_SERIAL	string	The serial of the server certificate
SSL_SERVER_S_DN	string	Subject DN in server's certificate
SSL_SERVER_S_DN_x509	string	Component of server's Subject DN
SSL_SERVER_I_DN	string	Issuer DN of server's certificate
SSL_SERVER_I_DN_x509	string	Component of server's Issuer DN
SSL_SERVER_V_START	string	Validity of server's certificate (start time)
SSL_SERVER_V_END	string	Validity of server's certificate (end time)
SSL_SERVER_A_SIG	string	Algorithm for the signature of server's certificate
SSL_SERVER_A_KEY	string	Algorithm for the public key of server's certificate
SSL_SERVER_CERT	string	PEM-encoded server certificate

[where x509 is a component of a X.509 DN: C,ST,L,O,OU,CN,T,I,G,S,D,UID,Email]

Your SSL configuration should look something like the following.

```
<IfModule mod_ssl.c>
        # Random Seeding
        SSLRandomSeed startup builtin
        SSLRandomSeed startup file:/dev/urandom 512
        SSLRandomSeed connect builtin
        SSLRandomSeed connect file:/dev/urandom 512

        # MIME configuration
        AddType application/x-x509-ca-cert .crt
        AddType application/x-pkcs7-crl .crl

    # How Apache configures dialogs in the terminal
    SSLPassPhraseDialog  exec:/usr/share/apache2/ask-for-passphrase

    # Session Caching
    SSLSessionCache            shmcb:${APACHE_RUN_DIR}/ssl_scache(512000)
    SSLSessionCacheTimeout  300

    # Encryption algorithms
    SSLCipherSuite HIGH:!aNULL
    SSLProtocol all -SSLv3
</IfModule>
```

Configuring the Secure Site in Apache

Now that you have the global SSL settings, you must tell Apache about the SSL server. This follows the form of a virtual host, which was covered in the previous chapter; in fact, Apache makes complete use of its virtual host functionality to configure SSL, and all directives used for virtual hosts are available for SSL servers. One difference, however, is that SSL-specific directives are included in the <VirtualHost> section.

The SSLEngine directive turns the SSL module on for this site; without this option set, you don't have a secure server. So don't forget this directive!

Next, you need to tell Apache where the certificate and certificate key files are. You should have noted these in the previous sections of this chapter. The SSLcertificateFile directive tells the server where the public certificate file is located.

If you remember, these files were obtained from Certbot and LetsEncrypt, or by becoming our own certificate authority, and placed in the `/etc/ssl` directory.

In the end, your site configuration file should look like the following.

```
<IfModule mod_ssl.c>
<VirtualHost *:443>
    DocumentRoot "/var/www/sites/local.apachebook.com"
    ServerName local.apachebook.com

    # Other directives here
    ErrorLog ${APACHE_LOG_DIR}/local.apachebook.com-error.log
    CustomLog ${APACHE_LOG_DIR}/local.apachebook.com-access.log combined

    # SSL Configuration
    Include /etc/letsencrypt/options-ssl-apache.conf
    SSLCertificateFile /etc/letsencrypt/live/local.apachebook.com-0001/
    fullchain.pem
    SSLCertificateKeyFile /etc/letsencrypt/live/local.apachebook.com-0001/
    privkey.pem
</VirtualHost>
</IfModule>
```

Once you have Apache configured and your server key and the public certificate installed, you can restart Apache and test your secure server. Test the server by loading it up using the `https://` prefix. For example, if your server existed at `http://local.apachebook.com`, you would load the secure server by loading `https://local.apachebook.com` in your browser.

If everything works well, you should see your page and a lock icon next to the URL in your browser window that indicates you are connected to a secure server.

Summing It Up

In this chapter, you learned about SSL and how to use it to secure your Apache web server. It covered securing your Apache web server easily through LetsEncrypt and Certbot and how to create a manual certificate for domains that LetsEncrypt can't reach.

You now know how to install the certificate on your computer or server and how to configure Apache for it.

The next chapter covers the last piece of Apache's configuration, log files. You learn about what they are, how to configure them in Apache, and how they can be useful for your projects.

CHAPTER 6

Log Files

In previous chapters, I discussed configuring several Apache features. But I haven't discussed *the most important* Apache feature you'll use: logging. Apache supplies two types of log files that track the activities of the Apache web server, ranging from errors encountered with the application and modules to pages requested by your website's users.

Log files are the bookkeepers of the server world. They're plain (text) and boring but of essential importance to daily operations. As you start working with Apache more often and consult log files regularly, you'll grow more comfortable with them, much like your bookkeeper.

Error.log

The `error.log` file archives all notices, warnings, and program errors encountered by Apache. This file can be safely ignored most of the time unless your web server is acting irrationally.

A standard entry in the error.log looks like the following.

```
[Fri Oct 3 06:25:11 2022] [notice] Apache/1.3.26 (Unix) Debian GNU/Linux
PHP/4.1.2 configured -- resuming normal operations
```

This line can be broken into three parts. The first part notes the log entry time, in this case, Friday, October 3, 2022, at 06:25:11. The second part indicates the log entry level: a notice. Finally, the line describes what happened: the server restarted.

Configuring the Error Log

To configure the error log, you need to specify two things: the file's location and the amount of information you want to place within it.

© Darren James Harkness 2022
D. J. Harkness, *Apache Essentials*, https://doi.org/10.1007/978-1-4842-8324-0_6

The first step is easy: simply tell it where you want to place the error log in `httpd.conf`. There is already an entry there that looks something like the following.

```
ErrorLog /var/log/apache/error.log
```

The next step is a little trickier. When configuring Apache, you can specify what level of entries to place within this log file. Table 6-1 lists the log levels in descending importance.

Table 6-1. *Apache Error Levels (`http://httpd.apache.org/docs/mod/core.html#loglevel`)*

Log Level	Description	Example
emerg	Emergency. The system is unusable. Anything that would cause Apache to quit unexpectedly or not load is logged as an emerg-level error.	"Child cannot open lock file. Exiting"
alert	Action must be taken immediately. These errors should be fixed as soon as possible but won't interfere with Apache's startup or shutdown. For example, if the server cannot determine its own domain name and switches over to its IP address.	"getpwuid: couldn't determine username from uid"
crit	Critical conditions. Errors marked critical indicate problems with Apache's normal operation. The example to the right shows that Apache attempted to open a socket (connection through which data is sent) and failed. These errors should be fixed relatively quickly when spotted.	"socket: failed to get a socket, exiting child.":

(continued)

Table 6-1. (*continued*)

Log Level	Description	Example
error	Error conditions indicating standard errors in operation but are still important. For example, if you have not configured the DocumentRoot an error condition appears, informing you that the directory does not exist. Often, CGI scripts can cause entries in the error.log, such as the one in the example.	"Premature end of script headers"
warn	Warning conditions. These aren't necessarily errors and usually indicate problems that Apache recovered from.	"child process 1234 did not exit, sending another SIGHUP"
notice	Normal but significant condition. These tend to be operational messages, such as Apache being started or stopped.	"httpd:caught SIGBUS, attempting to drop core in…"
info	Informational. Doesn't necessarily indicate an actual error. In the example to the right, Apache has noticed an increase in traffic above what it can handle and has logged the problem along with a solution.	"Server seems busy, (you may need to increase StartServers, or Min/MaxSpareServers)"
debug	Debug-level messages. This means everything.	"Opening config file…"

The further down the list you go for your LogLevel setting, the lengthier your error. log becomes. For example, a LogLevel of Debug is filled with much more information than a LogLevel of Crit. The Apache documentation recommends a LogLevel of Warn, and I agree.

You're likely to never look at error.log unless things start going drastically wrong. For production servers you should keep the file as small as possible. By selecting warn as your LogLevel, you can catch problems that may slow your web server down or cause it to not work.

For a development server, I recommend going right to debug as your LogLevel setting. Yes, this creates some larger log files over time. But it also gives you a *lot* of historical information that you can use for troubleshooting. I cover that in more depth in Chapter 7.

The format of the `LogLevel` looks like the following.

```
LogLevel warn
```

access.log

The access.log file contains a record of every single request sent to your Apache web server. For a single web page, several entries are often entered into the `access.log`: one for the web page itself, followed by one for each of the web page's support files (images, external CSS files, etc.). It'll take some time, but eventually, you'll have no problems following a thread through the log file.

Formatting the Access Log

The `LogFormat` and `CustomLog` directives format and create Apache log files. `LogFormat` sets up the contents of the log file. Multiple `LogFormat` entries are allowed but must have unique aliases.

The syntax of the `CustomLog` directive is the following.

```
LogFormat "<options>" <alias>
```

A sample `CustomLog` can be found in the default `httpd.conf`.

```
LogFormat "%h %l %u %t \"%r\" %>s %b \"%{Referer}i\" \"%{User-Agent}i\""
combined
```

Note   Double quotes must be escaped inside the LogFormat options. To escape the double quotes, use a backslash (for example, \").

Any text entered within the `LogFormat` directive's options appears in the log file. A full list of options can be seen in Table 6-2.

The default `httpd.conf` includes several pre-configured `LogFormat` aliases, including full, debug, combined, common, referrer, and agent. Most of the time, this is more than enough for you.

`CustomLog` tells Apache where to place the file and which `LogFormat` to use. The `CustomLog` uses the following syntax.

```
CustomLog /path/to/logfile alias
```

Table 6-2. *LogFormat Options*

Variable	Reports	Should you include it?
%a	The IP address making the HTTP request.	Yes. It's included in all the default log formats.
%A	Local IP address	Not really. You already know your IP address, which is not helpful when creating your site statistics. However, if you are running multiple servers, and combining the logs, this may be useful to tell you which server.
%B	Bytes sent to the browser, not including HTTP headers.	No. Although this is useful information, it is not in Common Log File (CLF) format. Instead, use %b.
%b	Bytes sent to the browser, not including HTTP headers. This attribute records the data in CLF format, however, recording a – instead of a 0 when no data is sent.	Yes. Transferring the amount of data is extremely important in generating site traffic statistics. Recording this data in CLF format ensures that any statistics package you use understands the information.
%c	Connection status when response was completed. The following are recorded. X means the connection was aborted before the response was completed. + means the connection may be kept alive after the response is sent. - means the connection closes after the response is sent.	No. This information is only useful for debugging problems with the web server.
%{VAR}e	Contents of the environment variable VAR.	No. Only use this if you need to store the contents of session variables to a log file outside of a scripted environment.
%f	Filename requested	No. This is included in the %r option.

(continued)

Table 6-2. (*continued*)

Variable	Reports	Should you include it?
%h	Remote Host	Yes.
%H	Request protocol	No. This is included in the %r option.
%{VAR}i	Displays the content of the specified header variable. Replace VAR with the header variable you want to display. For more information about header variables, consult `http://www.w3.org/Protocols/ HTTP/Object_Headers.html`. %{Referer}i is included in the default httpd.conf.	Yes, for specific information, such as referrers.
%l	The remote log name.	Yes, but only because it is included by default.
%m	The request method used by the browser.	No. This is included in the %r option.
%{VAR}n	The contents of a note from the specified module. Replace VAR with the name of the note.	No.
%{VAR}o	The contents of a specific header line in the server's reply. Replace VAR with the name of the header.	No. Only include this if you need specific information for debugging or troubleshooting.
%p	The port the web server is running on.	No. Only use this if you combine logs from servers running on different ports.
%P	The process ID of the Apache session that serviced the request.	No. This should only be used for troubleshooting purposes.
%q	The query string passed along with the URL. If no query string is passed, this returns no values.	No. This is included with the %r option.
%r	The first line of the incoming HTTP request. This includes the HTTP version, the request method, and the URL requested.	Yes. This is one of the more useful logging options.

(continued)

Table 6-2. (*continued*)

Variable	Reports	Should you include it?
%s	The status of the original request.	No. This reports the first request made, including forwarded pages. Use %>s instead.
%>s	The status of the last request.	Yes.
%t	The time in CLF that the request was made. The CLF time format looks like the following. [07/Dec/2021:13:15:32 -0700]	Yes.
%{format} t	Use this option to change the time format. The available time formats are viewable at `http://unixhelp.ed.ac.uk/CGI/man-cgi?strftime+3`.	No. Only change this if you require a standard time format that is different from the one supplied by the %t option.
%T	The time taken to serve the request, in seconds.	No. This is only useful for server / script benchmarks.
%u	Remote user name. This is the person logged in to your web server via htaccess.	Yes, but only because it's included by default. This option is also useful if you are using htaccess to restrict access to directories on your web server.
%U	The URL requested, not including the query string. For example, if the requested URL was /scripts/search.php?keyword=foobar, the value returned by the %U option would be /scripts/search.php.	No. The %r option covers this.
%v	The name of the Apache server.	No. Only use this if you are combining log files and need to know the name of the server.
%V	The name of the Apache server, according to the UseCanonicalName setting.	No. Only use this if you are combining log files and need to know the name of the server.

An example of this would be the following.

```
CustomLog /var/log/apache/access.log combined
```

This would write a log entry to the file /var/log/apache/access.log using the combined LogFormat mentioned earlier. You can create multiple CustomLog entries, but each must point to a unique file to avoid conflicts.

As you can see, the default CustomLog and LogFormat directives are pretty useful. However, you may want to change the log entry format to better suit your purposes. For example, you may want to change the LogFormat to include a comma as a delimiter between the parts of a log file for easier importing into Excel. Or, you may want to change the order of elements within the entry or add information not included by default. To do so, use the options in Table 6-2 to create your own CustomLog file directives in httpd.conf.

Caution   Changing the default LogFormat string can have undesirable effects, especially if you are using software to analyze and create statistics on your website. Only change this if you're *really* certain that you want to and you know the effects it has.

At first glance, Apache's log files are pretty intimidating. There is a lot of information recorded in each log file in a very compressed format. However, when you break it down into recognizable parts, it becomes much easier to understand. Each entry in the access. log contains a wealth of information; it's just a matter of learning how to read it.

The following is a fairly typical entry in the access.log.

```
70.68.89.139 - darren [15/May/2022:13:17:48 -0700] "GET /contact.php
HTTP/1.1" 404 5265 "https://local.apachebook.com/" "Mozilla/5.0 (Macintosh;
Intel Mac OS X 10_15_7) AppleWebKit/605.1.15 (KHTML, like Gecko)
Version/15.4 Safari/605.1.15".
```

Figure 6-1 breaks this down into recognizable parts.

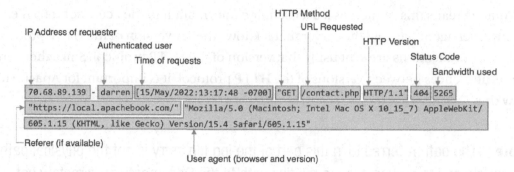

Figure 6-1. Breaking down a log file entry

`70.68.89.139`

This is the IP the request originated from. Often, this field contains a hostname instead of an IP address; for example, `staticred.net` or `dialh2434.someprovider.net`. Knowing the IP address or hostname is extremely important for tracking user visits, paths taken through the site, and so on.

This is a spot reserved for the Apache server's IP address. This is not recorded by default. It's generally used when combining multiple Apache log files into a single log file (often for load balancers).

`darren`

This is the authenticated user who requested the page. This should only be recorded if a user has authenticated him or herself through Apache before requesting the page. Once they have authenticated on the Apache server, their username is recorded with every request they make. Refer to the section in the Chapter 2, where I discussed the .htaccess and .htpasswd files for more information.

In this case, the "darren" user requested the page. Hey, that name looks familiar.

`[15/May/2022:13:17:48 -0700]`

This is the date the request was made, recorded down to the second.

`"GET /contact.php HTTP/1.1"`

This is the request method, page, and HTTP version sent to Apache from the browser. In this case, a GET request was made for contact.php by a browser using version 1.1 of the HTTP protocol.

Apache reads this request as a user sending information to the `/contact.php` file. The browser agent has told the server that it knows the 1.1 version of the HTTP protocol, so all communications are sent using that version of the HTTP protocol. Since there are minor differences between versions of the HTTP protocol, it is important for Apache to know this.

Note   The path referred to in this part of the log file entry is not the physical path of the file on the server. It is the relative path to the DocumentRoot directory set up in your httpd.conf file for the domain. For example, if your DocumentRoot was configured to be /var/www, the file accessed would *actually* exist at `/var/www/contact.php`. It seems like a minor point, but I've known a few people to be confused by this.

`200`

This is the HTTP code sent to the browser. In this case, the file requested exists on the server, so a code 200 (OK) is sent to the browser. If the file did not exist, a 404 would be recorded. For more information on HTTP error codes, refer to the list of HTTP status codes in the Appendix.

`41418`

The number of bytes transferred to the browser is also recorded for statistics. In this case, the script sent 41,418 bytes of information. This part of the log entry can be very useful for troubleshooting scripts or calculating the amount of data transferred for a given period or file.

`"https://local.apachebook.com"`

This field shows the referrer or page that directed the client to this request. In this example, you can see that the user loaded the home page and has opened the contact form (`contact.php`).

This field simply shows a hyphen if there is no referrer (otherwise known as a *direct request*). Direct requests are often common for graphic files, flash files, or any other file type included in a web page.

```
"Mozilla/5.0 (Macintosh; Intel Mac OS X 10_15_7) AppleWebKit/605.1.15
(KHTML, like Gecko) Version/15.4 Safari/605.1.15"
```

The user agent (the user's browser and version) is the final piece of log entry puzzle. In the example entry, the user is viewing the site in Safari 15.4 on macOS 10.15.7.

Obtaining the user agent is very helpful when auditing the site design and code. If you know that 95% of your users are viewing the site with newer browsers, you can take advantage of technologies supported by those browsers. Likewise, if 25% of your users are still using older browsers that don't support the newer technologies, you know ahead of time that you should rethink using them.

This section gets a bit sticky since it's one of the few pieces of information sent directly from the browser. Some browser manufacturers don't identify themselves or identify themselves as another browser. For example, the Opera browser can be configured to identify itself as Opera, Mozilla, or several versions of Internet Explorer.

Where Can I Find Apache's Log Files?

The location of Apache's log files is configurable within the httpd.conf file and can vary if you run multiple sites on a single Apache server. Generally, however, you can find the files in the default log directory. On a Linux system, they can be found in the /var/log/apache directory. On macOS, they are in /usr/local/logs/httpd. On a Windows system, they can be found in C:\xampp\apache\logs.

Configuring Apache Logs

By default, Apache's logging is pretty good; it keeps a basic level of information about the Apache executable in the error.log and tracks most client information in the access.log. You'll likely not have to change the default settings for logging. That is, until something goes wrong.

I'll save you a throbbing headache later and show you how to configure logging to capture problems before they become unsolvable. We'll focus on the directives listed in Table 6-3.

Table 6-3. *Details the Directives Used When Configuring Apache Log Files*

Directive	Function
HostNameLookups	Configures Apache to look up the hostname for a given IP address and record it in the log files.
ErrorLog	Configures the name and the location of Apache's error log. This log records all activities of the Apache application, depending on which LogLevel is set.
LogLevel	Configures the detail to include in the Apache error log.
LogFormat	Configures which information is included in Apache's access logs. Multiple LogFormats can be configured, each with its own unique alias.
CustomLog	Configures the file location and LogFormat to use. Multiple CustomLog entries can be configured.

Log Files for Virtual Hosts

If you are running multiple domains from a single Apache web server, creating separate logs for each domain is a good idea. Although you can place everything into a single log file, it's generally not a good idea. With the standard access.log LogFormat, there are no identifying marks to determine which domains were accessed in any given entry.

A good convention to follow is to prefix each log's file name with the domain name. For example, the `apachebook.local` log files are `apachebook.local_access.log` and `apachebook.local_error.log`. This way, you can easily access log files for a specific name without searching through a monolithic log file.

For more information on virtual hosts, refer to Chapter 3.

Rotating Logs

As information is written to Apache's log files, they can rapidly grow to an unwieldy size. Since Apache records every access to the website, it likely records tens of thousands of lines of data daily. The more information recorded and supporting files it uses in a site's design, the more lines Apache writes to the log files.

A strategy to handle the problem of file size is to enable rotating log files in Apache. Rotating the log files allows you to maintain several smaller log files, which automatically archive themselves. Beyond the first archive, the files are often archived to save space.

The archived files keep the same filename but have a number appended to them that grows with their age. For example, the newest archive file would be access.log if you had ten archive files.0, while the oldest would be `access.log.9.gz`.

I recommend keeping about a year's worth of log files at any given time. Log files after that point aren't very useful for gathering information about your website beyond comparison purposes. If you want to keep all your web logs, simply back them up to an alternate location once every month or so.

Configuring Log Rotation

Older versions of Apache configured log rotation within the `httpd.conf` file. However, recent versions use a third-party application called logrotate. This is installed by default on most Linux distributions using Apache and makes the rotation of logs quite simple. logrotate is configured through the `/etc/logrotate.d/apache` file.

Note   logrotate is not installed on macOS or Windows.

A sample logrotate configuration file for Apache looks like the following.

```
/var/log/apache/*.log {
    weekly
    missingok
    rotate 52
    compress
    delaycompress
    notifempty
    create 640 root adm
    sharedscripts
    postrotate
        /etc/init.d/apache reload > /dev/null
    endscript
}
```

Let's break this down. The first line tells logrotate where to find the log files. In this case, it's being told to look in /var/log/apache for all files with a .log extension. It then opens the options directives with an open curly bracket ({).

```
/var/log/apache/*.log {
```

The next lines indicate which options to set for logrotate. These options are outlined in Table 6-4.

Table 6-4. *logrotate Configuration File Options (`http://www.die.net/doc/ linux/man/man8/logrotate.8.html`)*

Option	Description
compress	Old versions of log files are compressed with gzip by default. See also **nocompress**.
compresscmd	Specifies which command to use to compress log files. The default is gzip. See also compress.
uncompresscmd	Specifies which command to use to uncompress log files. The default is **gunzip**.
compressext	Specifies which extension to use on compressed log files, if compression is enabled. The default follows that of the configured compression command.
compressoptions	Command line options may be passed to the compression program, if one is in use. The default, for gzip, is "-9" (maximum compression).
copy	Make a copy of the log file, but don't change the original. For instance, this option can be used to make a snapshot of the current log file or when some other utility needs to truncate or parse the file. When this option is used, the create option has no effect because the old log file stays in place.

(continued)

Table 6-4. (*continued*)

Option	Description
copytruncate	Truncate the original log file in place after creating a copy, instead of moving the old log file and optionally creating a new one, It can be used when some program can not be told to close its log file and thus might continue writing (appending) to the previous log file forever. Note that there is a very small time slice between copying and truncating the file, so some logging data might be lost. When this option is used, the create option has no effect because the old log file stays in place.
create mode owner group	Immediately after rotation (before the postrotate script is run), the log file is created (with the same name as the log file just rotated). mode specifies the mode for the log file in octal (the same as chmod(2)), owner specifies the user name who owns the log file, and group specifies the group the log file belongs to. Any log file attributes may be omitted, in which case those attributes for the new file use the same values as the original log file for the omitted attributes. This option can be disabled using the nocreate option.
daily	Log files are rotated every day.
delaycompress	Postpone compression of the previous log file to the next rotation cycle. This has only effect when used in combination with compress. It can be used when some program can not be told to close its log file and thus might continue writing to the previous log file for some time.
extension *ext*	Log files are given the final extension ext after rotation. If compression is used, the compression extension (normally .gz) appears after ext.
ifempty	Rotate the log file even if it is empty, overriding the notifempty option (ifempty is the default).

(*continued*)

Table 6-4. (*continued*)

Option	Description
include file_or_directory	Reads the file given as an argument as if it was included inline where the include directive appears. If a directory is given, most of the files in that directory are read in alphabetic order before processing of the including file continues. The only files which are ignored are files that are not regular files (such as directories and named pipes) and files whose names end with one of the taboo extensions, as specified by the tabooext directive. The include directive may not appear inside of a log file definition.
mail *address*	When a log is rotated out of existence, it is mailed to the address. If a particular log should generate no mail, the nomail directive may be used.
mailfirst	When using the mail command, mail the just-rotated file instead of the about-to-expire file.
maillast	When using the mail command, mail the about-to-expire file instead of the just-rotated file. (This is the default.)
missingok	If the log file is missing, go on to the next without issuing an error message. See also nomissingok.
monthly	Log files are rotated the first time logrotate is run in a month. (This is normally on the first day of the month.)
nocompress	Old versions of log files are not compressed with gzip. See also compress.
nocopy	Do not copy the original log file and leave it in place. (This overrides the copy option.)
nocopytruncate	Do not truncate the original log file after creating a copy. (This overrides the copytruncate option.)
nocreate	New log files are not created. (This overrides the create option.)
nodelaycompress	Do not postpone the compression of the previous log file to the next rotation cycle. (This overrides the delaycompress option.)

(*continued*)

Table 6-4. (*continued*)

Option	Description
nomail	Don't mail old log files to any address.
nomissingok	If a log file does not exist, issue an error. This is the default.
noolddir	Logs are rotated in the same directory the log normally resides in. (This overrides the **olddir** option.)
nosharedscripts	Run **prerotate** and **postrotate** scripts for every rotated script. (This is the default and overrides the **sharedscripts** option.)
notifempty	Do not rotate the log if it is empty. (This overrides the **ifempty** option.)
olddir directory	Logs are moved into the directory for rotation. The directory must be on the same physical device as the rotated log file. When this option is used, all old versions of the log end up in the directory. This option may be overridden by the **noolddir** option.
postrotate/endscript	The lines between *postrotate* and *endscript* (both of which must appear on lines by themselves) are executed after the log file is rotated. These directives may only appear inside of a log file definition. Also see **prerotate**.
prerotate/endscript	The lines between **prerotate** and **endscript** (both of which must appear on lines by themselves) are executed before the log file is rotated and only if the log is actually rotated. These directives may only appear inside of a log file definition. Also see **postrotate**.
rotate count	The lines between **prerotate** and **endscript** (both of which must appear on lines by themselves) are executed before the log file is rotated and only if the log is actually rotated. These directives may only appear inside of a log file definition. Also see **postrotate**.

(*continued*)

Table 6-4. (*continued*)

Option	Description
size size	The lines between prerotate and endscript (both of which must appear on lines by themselves) are executed before the log file is rotated and only if the log is rotated. These directives may only appear inside of a log file definition. Also see **postrotate**.
sharedscripts	Normally, **prescript** and **postscript** scripts are run for each rotated log, meaning that a single script may be run multiple times for log entries that match multiple files (such as the /var/log/news/* example). If **sharedscript** is specified, the scripts are only run once, no matter how many logs match the wildcarded pattern. However, if none of the logs in the pattern require rotating, the scripts do not run at all. This option overrides the nosharedscripts option.
start count	This is the number to use as the base for rotation. For example, if you specify 0, the logs are created with a .0 extension as they are rotated from the original log files. If you specify 9, log files are created with a .9, skipping 0 to 8. Files are still rotated the number of times specified with the **count** directive.
tabooext [+] list	The current taboo extension list has been changed (see the **include** directive for information on the taboo extensions). If a + precedes the list of extensions, the current taboo extension list is augmented; otherwise, it is replaced. At startup, the taboo extension list contains .rpmorig, .rpmsave, ,v, .swp, .rpmnew, and ~.
weekly	Log files are rotated if the current weekday is less than the weekday of the last rotation or if more than a week has passed since the last rotation. This is normally the same as rotating logs on the first day of the week, but it works better if *logrotate* is not run every night.

If you are a Windows user or don't have access to logrotate, you can use piped logs. Apache ships with an application called rotatelogs, a more basic version of logrotate that doesn't support compression. An example entry in `httpd.conf` for rotatelogs would look like the following.

```
TransferLog "|rotatelogs /path/to/logs/access.log 86400"
```

This would pass the contents of the access.log file once every 24 hours.

TIP   You can also specify a file size for the rotatelog command instead of specifying a time in seconds. To rotate a log once it reaches 5 megabytes, the directive would be: TransferLog "|rotatelogs /path/to/logs/access.log 5M".

Reading Archived Log Files

To save space, archived log files are often compressed using the gzip compression scheme. To read them, you must either uncompress their contents or use a text editor that supports reading gzipped files.

On Linux and macOS, you can read gzipped text files using the vi editor, which is installed by default on most systems. You can search through them using the `zgrep` command, which is identical to the `grep` command.

With Windows, you must uncompress the archived files to a temporary directory using a program such as WinZip.

What Do I Do with Log Files?

You can do several things with Apache's log files beyond taking up disk space. Apache's log files can be used for troubleshooting, which is covered in Chapter 7, and for site analytics. You do not need to rely on Google Analytics and Tag Manager to analyze your website traffic, and you're better off from a privacy standpoint if you move away from Google's tools.

Apache's log files are a very useful resource for creating statistics on your website. Because the access.log records every piece of available information, log files can determine your site's usage, traffic patterns, where your visitors are coming from, or missing pages.

As you've already seen, unless you've been a bad reader and skipped ahead, the access.log records pretty much anything and everything you'll ever want to know. You have access to pages requested, files sent, kilobytes transferred, browsers used, and much, much more. It's marketing gold: not only can you see what your clients are looking at, but how they got there, which browser they used to view it, how long they spent browsing other pages, and in some cases, even the geographical region they were browsing from.

By aggregating and analyzing all this data, you can better direct the content development of your website, create marketing plans that effectively target members of your audience and use technologies that are supported by the browsers your clients use. It's all a question of how to aggregate and analyze the data.

Using Log Analysis Programs

The raw log files are strongly beneficial, but they're a nightmare when doing anything useful with them. A standard entry, as you have already seen, contains a large amount of information; now, consider the entries for support files and multiply that by hundreds or thousands of entries a day. It quickly becomes an untamed beast, and unless you're some kind of mathematical god able to remember and process massive amounts of information, trying to make any sense of all that information becomes impossible very quickly.

This is why Google Analytics has become such a popular solution for tracking and analyzing website traffic. Of course, you're also giving up your and your users' information with every site visit. That doesn't have to be the case, however. Using one of the following tools, you can easily generate your own site analytics directly from Apache's log files.

- ApacheViewer

- AWStats

- Loggly

- New Relic

- Webalizer (old but robust)

This lets you control your and your users' data while providing useful information about how the website is being used.

Creating Custom Scripts

Sometimes, a log analysis package won't always fit your needs. I discovered this a few months ago when I needed the ability to search my log files for a specific term. I already knew enough PHP to get myself into trouble, so I decided it would be faster and more efficient if I wrote a script to do it for me instead of searching through Google results.

One of the benefits of the script I wrote was that I could use the same search functionality to track users' paths through the site. I simply had to search the logs for their hostname. The script I used is as follows (you can find a fully commented, nicer-looking version of this script at the Apress website).

```
<?php
$filename="/var/log/apache/access.log"; // location of the log file -
configure this
?>
<HTML>
<head>
<title>apache log search form<?if ($searchterm) {echo ":
$searchterm";}?></title>
</head>
<body>
if ($searchterm) { ?>
<b>Searching for:</b> <? echo "$searchterm<br><br>"; ?>
<div class="results">
<? $entry = array();
$entry = file($filename) or die("Cannot open file");
$fillval = count($entry);
$entry = array_merge($entry);
$i=0;
foreach ($entry as $si) {
if (ereg($searchterm,$si) & !ereg(".css",$si) & !ereg(".jpg",$si) &
!ereg("search.php",$si)) {
$lineval = explode(" ",$si);
echo "<b>Site:</b> <a href=\"/scripts/search.php?searchterm=$lineval[0]\">$
lineval[0]</a> (click to show path through site)<br>";
```

```
echo "<b>URL:</b> <a href=\"/scripts/search.php?searchterm=$lineval[6]\">$l
ineval[6]</a> (click to see what other sites have hit this URL)<br>";
$lineval[10] = ereg_replace(chr(34),"",$lineval[10]);
if ($lineval[10] != "-") {
            echo "<b>Referer:</b> <a href=\"$lineval[10]\">$lineval[10]</
            a> &#187; <a href=\"/scripts/search.php?searchterm=$lineval[1
            0]\">search this term</a><br>";
        }
        else {
        echo "<b>Direct Request</b><br>";
        }
        echo "<b>Browser:</b> $lineval[11] $lineval[12] $lineval[13]
        $lineval[14] $lineval[15] $lineval[16] $lineval[17]<br/>";
        echo "<b>Date:</b> $lineval[3]$lineval[4]";
        echo "<hr>";
    $i++;
    }
  }
echo "<br><br>Number of entries: $i &#187; ";
}
?>
<form action="/scripts/search.php">
Search for term: <input type="text" name="searchterm" class="send"> <input
type="submit" class="send" value=" &#187; ">
</form>
</body>
</html>
```

Note   Before you use this script, you need to specify the location of your log files in the $filename variable.

Troubleshooting Apache

You can also use the Apache logs to troubleshoot problems with scripts and Apache itself.

Apache Configuration

Hopefully, you've been using `sudo apachectl configtest` when modifying your Apache configuration. You're human, so chances are good you forgot, and now your Apache server won't start up. Or perhaps you put a local .htaccess file in place on one of your development servers, and the site is now reporting a 500 error. Fortunately, Apache's logging has your back.

Any issues that Apache encounters with its configuration are always reported to the error log. For example, if you were configuring basic authentication on your dev site using a `.htaccess` file, enter the following without first creating the `.htpasswd` file.

```
AuthType Basic
AuthName "Authentication Required"
AuthUserFile ".htpasswd"
Require valid-user
```

When attempting to load the dev site, the browser would ask for a username and password and then report an internal server error. By looking in the error log, you could see the following.

```
[Sun Apr 24 10:18:16.513809 2022] [authn_file:error] [pid 440770] (2)No
such file or directory: [client 70.68.89.139:57410] AH01620: Could not open
password file: /etc/apache2/.htpasswd
```

This tells you a couple of things. First, the `.htaccess` configuration refers to a password file that does not exist (`/etc/apache2/.htpasswd`). Second, Apache is looking in `/etc/apache` for the `.htpasswd` file instead of in the dev site's directory.

This would give you all the information needed to fix the issue. First, you need to create the `.htpassword` file. Open your terminal and enter the following (using the path to your own dev site's location).

```
htpasswd -c /Users/reader/sites/dev.local/.htpasswd reader
```

You'll be asked to enter a password for the user.

```
New password:
Re-type new password:
Adding password for user reader
```

Once that's complete, update the .htaccess file to point to the correct location of the .htpasswd file.

```
AuthType Basic
AuthName "Authentication Required"
AuthUserFile "/Users/reader/sites/dev.local/.htpasswd"
Require valid-user
```

Tracking Down 404 Errors and Why They Occur

Perhaps one of the most useful troubleshooting capabilities of Apache's log files is tracking down 404 errors (missing files) on your website and finding where they were referred from. In Chapter 5, I discussed the structure of a log file entry for a successful page view. The structure of the log file is nearly identical to the missing files. The only difference is that a 404 is recorded instead of a 200 for the HTTP result code.

Because the entry in the access.log is recorded identically for a missing file as it is for an existing file, all the information about the request is available, including a referrer. (Can you see where I'm going with this?) As a result, you can see where the page request originated. If the page request originated on your server, you know exactly where to go to fix the problem.

Because you know the result code for a missing file, you could even write a script to search for missing files in your Apache logs and report which requests are spawning 404 errors and where they are coming from.

Troubleshooting PHP

The Apache logs are *always* the first place to look when a website is not acting the way you expect. Modern content management systems and development frameworks put all sorts of information into Apache's log files to help developers debug issues.

The following is an example of a fatal script error and what you can learn from it.

```
error.local-error.log.1:[Wed Oct 06 15:40:47.879597 2021] [php7:error] [pid
770418] [client 192.168.1.173:60963] PHP Fatal error:  Uncaught Error: Call
to undefined function curl_init() in /var/www/sites/errors/src/curl-call.
php:100\nStack trace:\n#0 /var/www/sites/errors/src/curl-call.php(41):
get_book_list_for_author()\n#1 /var/www/sites/errors/src/curl-call.php(18):
```

```
author_list_no_handling_errors()\n#2 {main}\n  thrown in /var/www/sites/
errors/src/curl-call.php on line 100, referer: http://errors.local/
```

This was from a tutorial package I was writing for the dev team at my agency that was intended to help them work through the use of error handling. However, when I placed this on my local server, it wasn't working at all. When I looked through the error logs, it became quickly apparent what the problem was the following.

```
PHP Fatal error:  Uncaught Error: Call to undefined function curl_init()
```

From this, I could tell that PHP had not been configured to enable the cURL module, which includes the `curl_init()` function. Without this module being enabled in PHP, that function (and all other cURL functions) simply isn't available.

Writing to the Error Log

Not every problem encountered by PHP is logged, unfortunately. Often, there are issues with external services, formatting, or logic that cause a script to fail, despite having syntactically correct PHP. When that happens, you need to debug your scripts, going through them step by step to determine where the issue is being introduced.

One powerful way of debugging your PHP scripts is to write information to the error logs. PHP provides two functions to support this: `error_log()` and `trigger_error()`. Both are similar; however, `error_log()` writes an entry to the Apache error logs regardless of how PHP is configured. In contrast, `trigger_error()` depends on how PHP is configured to record error messages (to screen, log file, or both).

I recommend using `error_log()` for most cases since it records the error in a more permanent manner, making it easier to track errors over time.

An Example

Let's say you're having issues writing to an API, which is expecting a JSON payload to follow a very specific format. Here's an example of a PHP script that sends a message through the Slack API.

```php
<?php
// Grab form data
$name = isset($_POST['name']) ? $_POST['name'] : null;
$email = isset($_POST['email']) ? $_POST['email'] : null;
```

```php
$about = isset($_POST['about']) ? $_POST['about'] : null;

$webhook = "https://hooks.slack.com/services/<webhookid>";

// Prepare the payload
$payload = [
  "text" => "Incoming lead",
  "blocks" => [
      [
        "type" => "header",
        "text" => [
          "type" => "plain_text",
          "text" => "Incoming Lead",
          "emoji" => true
      ],[
          "type" => "section",
          "text" => [
            "type" => "mrkdwn",
            "text" => sprintf("*%s* is curious about Apache and would
            like to know more about *%s*. You can reach out to them at
            %s",$name,$about,$email),
          ]
        ]
      ]
  ],
];

$json = json_encode($payload);
$curl = curl_init($webhook);
curl_setopt($curl, CURLOPT_HEADER, TRUE);
curl_setopt($curl, CURLOPT_RETURNTRANSFER, true);
curl_setopt($curl, CURLOPT_HTTPHEADER, array("Content-type: application/
json"));
curl_setopt($curl, CURLOPT_POST, true);
curl_setopt($curl, CURLOPT_POSTFIELDS, $json);
$json_response = curl_exec($curl);
$errors = curl_error($curl);
```

```
$status = curl_getinfo($curl, CURLINFO_HTTP_CODE);
$json = json_decode($json_response);
```

When the script sends this JSON payload to the API, it returns an invalid_blocks_format error about the JSON format for the blocks array. This is odd because that's how a multidimensional array should look. It's clear that the API isn't receiving things in the format it's expecting.

To help debug this, I made use of the error_log() function to record the contents of the $json variable before it is sent, so I know exactly what's going to the API. It looks like the following.

```
$json = json_encode($payload);
$error_log("Here's what I'm sending: {$json}");
$curl = curl_init($webhook);
```

The following is what comes back.

```
[20-May-2022 23:29:41 UTC] Here's what I'm sending: {"text":"Incoming lead
","blocks":[{"type":"header","text":{"type":"plain_text","text": "Incoming
Lead","emoji":true},"0":{"type":"section","text":          {"type":"mrkdwn",
"text":"*Darren* is curious about Apache and would like to know more about
*Configuring it*. You can reach out to them at someone@somewhere.com"}}}]}
```

As it turns out, the JSON is not following the format Slack's API expects. The json_encode() function adds an index of 0 in the second entry in the array that shouldn't be there.

As it turns out, this is a weird gotcha with json_encode() and multidimensional arrays. I need to define it a little differently. First, a multidimensional array needs to be created and added to the payload separately.

```
$blocks[] = [
    "type" => "header",
    "text" => [
      "type" => "plain_text",
      "text" => "Incoming Lead",
      "emoji" => true
    ],
  ];
$blocks[] = [
    "type" => "section",
```

```
    "text" => [
      "type" => "mrkdwn",
      "text" => sprintf("*%s* is curious about Apache and would
      like to know more about *%s*. You can reach out to them at
      %s",$name,$about,$email),
    ]
  ];

$payload = [
  "text" => "Incoming lead",
  "blocks" => $blocks,
];
```

Once I've made this change and tested it, I get the JSON payload in the format the Slack API expects.

```
[20-May-2022 16:16:48 America/Vancouver] {"text":"Incoming lead",  "blocks
":[{"type":"header","text":{"type":"plain_text","text":"Incoming Lead","em
oji":true}},{"type":"section","text":{"type":"mrkdwn","text": "*Darren* is
curious about Apache and would like to know more about *web development*.
You can reach out to them at hello@apachebook.com"}}]}
```

And now that I know it's working, I can remove the error_log() from the script as it's no longer needed.

I couldn't have debugged this script without using the error log because the API works over a cURL session instead of writing to the screen. There isn't an opportunity to see what's going there, so we must capture it and send the data elsewhere.

Summing It Up

Apache's logging is an extremely powerful tool for troubleshooting website issues and managing site analytics. Combining Apache's logging with PHP's debugging capabilities makes it simple to track down issues quickly and easily. Using server-side analytics tools like AWStats or ApacheViewer gives you control over your site's usage data without having to share it with third-party processors such as Google.

The next chapter covers some sample Apache configurations, which you can use to quickly spin up your own development instances.

CHAPTER 7

Sample Apache Configurations

This chapter sets up several scenarios and shows you how to best configure Apache to handle each one. I set this up in an anecdotal format because, well, it's a heck of a lot more interesting to read.

The following examples assume you are using macOS. You may have to adjust the directories for Windows to suit your local installation. If you are using Linux, note that you need to break these up to fit into the `mods-enabled` and `sites-enabled` directory structure.

Don't worry about typing these all out by hand. A repository of Apache configurations is at `https://github.com/staticred/apache-essentials`.

Basic Apache Configuration (with PHP)

Let's start with the most basic of Apache configurations: a local development website reachable at `http://localhost/`.

For this configuration, you only need to worry about editing the `httpd.conf` or `apache.conf` file to configure a single site in Apache.

httpd.conf

```
# +---------------------+
# | Basic configuration |
# +---------------------+

# ServerRoot: The top of the directory tree under which the server's
# configuration, error, and log files are kept. This example is for
```

© Darren James Harkness 2022
D. J. Harkness, *Apache Essentials*, https://doi.org/10.1007/978-1-4842-8324-0_7

```
# MacOS using Homebrew to install Apache.
ServerRoot "/usr/local/opt/httpd"

# Listen: Allows you to bind Apache to specific IP addresses and/or
# ports, instead of the default. See also the <VirtualHost>
# directive.
Listen 80

# Set up a separate user for the Apache process to run under. This
# protects your system from running with escalated privileges that
# malicious code can take advantage of.
<IfModule unixd_module>
User _www
Group _www
</IfModule>

# +-----------------+
# | Apache Modules  |
# +-----------------+
LoadModule mpm_prefork_module lib/httpd/modules/mod_mpm_prefork.so
LoadModule authn_file_module lib/httpd/modules/mod_authn_file.so
LoadModule authn_core_module lib/httpd/modules/mod_authn_core.so
LoadModule authz_host_module lib/httpd/modules/mod_authz_host.so
LoadModule authz_groupfile_module lib/httpd/modules/mod_authz_groupfile.so
LoadModule authz_user_module lib/httpd/modules/mod_authz_user.so
LoadModule authz_core_module lib/httpd/modules/mod_authz_core.so
LoadModule access_compat_module lib/httpd/modules/mod_access_compat.so
LoadModule auth_basic_module lib/httpd/modules/mod_auth_basic.so
LoadModule reqtimeout_module lib/httpd/modules/mod_reqtimeout.so
LoadModule filter_module lib/httpd/modules/mod_filter.so
LoadModule mime_module lib/httpd/modules/mod_mime.so
LoadModule log_config_module lib/httpd/modules/mod_log_config.so
LoadModule env_module lib/httpd/modules/mod_env.so
LoadModule headers_module lib/httpd/modules/mod_headers.so
LoadModule setenvif_module lib/httpd/modules/mod_setenvif.so
LoadModule version_module lib/httpd/modules/mod_version.so
LoadModule unixd_module lib/httpd/modules/mod_unixd.so
```

```
LoadModule status_module lib/httpd/modules/mod_status.so
LoadModule autoindex_module lib/httpd/modules/mod_autoindex.so
LoadModule dir_module lib/httpd/modules/mod_dir.so
LoadModule alias_module lib/httpd/modules/mod_alias.so
LoadModule rewrite_module lib/httpd/modules/mod_rewrite.so

# +--------------+
# | PHP Config   |
# +--------------+
LoadModule php_module /usr/local/opt/php@8.0/lib/httpd/modules/libphp.so
<FilesMatch \.php$>
  SetHandler application/x-httpd-php
</FilesMatch>

# +-----------------------------+
# | 'Main' server configuration |
# +-----------------------------+
#
# The directives in this section set up the values used by the 'main'
# server, which responds to any requests that aren't handled by a
# <VirtualHost> definition.  These values also provide defaults for
# any <VirtualHost> containers you may define later in the file.
#
# All of these directives may appear inside <VirtualHost> containers,
# in which case these default settings will be overridden for the
# virtual host being defined.

# Your email address, where problems with the server should be emailed.
# This might be exposed to users on some error pages.
ServerAdmin you@example.com

# The domain or subdomain name of your primary Apache server and port.
# Since we're setting up our local host, we'll call it 'localhost',
# which is a reserved host name.
ServerName localhost:80

# Let's protect our system's files from being accessed outside of
# our site directories.
```

```
<Directory />
    AllowOverride none
    Require all denied
</Directory>

# +----------------------------+
# | Primary site configuration |
# +----------------------------+

# Where the files for the primary website live on your computer.
DocumentRoot "/Users/darren/sites/localhost"
<Directory "/Users/darren/sites/localhost">
    #
    # Possible values for the Options directive are "None", "All",
    # or any combination of:
    #    Indexes Includes FollowSymLinks SymLinksifOwnerMatch ExecCGI
      MultiViews
    #
    # Note that "MultiViews" must be named *explicitly* --- "Options All"
    # doesn't give it to you.
    #
    # The Options directive is both complicated and important.  Please see
    # http://httpd.apache.org/docs/2.4/mod/core.html#options
    # for more information.
    #
    # Set up our options to allow the site to create indexes of files in
    # the browser if a directory is loaded without an index.php or
      index.html,
    # and to allow Apache to load files added through a symbolic link.
    Options Indexes FollowSymLinks

    # Allow the use of .htaccess to allow custom directives to be
      added without
    # restarting Apache.
    AllowOverride All

    # Controls who can get stuff from this server.
```

```
    Require all granted
</Directory>

# Look for index.php and display it. If there is no index.php, look for an
# index.html instead. If nothing found, Apache will show an index of files
# in the directory.
<IfModule dir_module>
    DirectoryIndex index.php index.html
</IfModule>

# Prevent any file starting with .ht from being displayed on the
website. (e.g.,
# .htaccess or .htpasswd)
<Files ".ht*">
    Require all denied
</Files>

# +----------------------+
# | Logging configuration |
# +----------------------+

# Specifies the default location of your error log. Any Virtualhosts later
# defined will default to using this logfile if no other ErrorLog
location is
# specified.
ErrorLog "/usr/local/var/log/httpd/error_log"

# Tells Apache how detailed to be with its logging. Since this is a
development
# server, we'll set it to debug, the most informative setting. For
production
# servers, you would want to change this to warn instead.
LogLevel debug

# Configure logging formats
<IfModule log_config_module>
    #
    # The following directives define some format nicknames for use with
```

```
    # a CustomLog directive (see below).
    LogFormat "%h %l %u %t \"%r\" %>s %b \"%{Referer}i\" \"%{User-Agent}
    i\"" combined
    LogFormat "%h %l %u %t \"%r\" %>s %b" common

    <IfModule logio_module>
      # You need to enable mod_logio.c to use %I and %O
      LogFormat "%h %l %u %t \"%r\" %>s %b \"%{Referer}i\" \"%{User-Agent}
      i\" %I %O" combinedio
    </IfModule>

    # Specifies the default location of your access log. Any
      Virtualhosts later
    # defined will default to using this logfile if no other CustomLog
      location
    # is specified.
    CustomLog "/usr/local/var/log/httpd/access_log" common
</IfModule>

# +-------------------+
# | CGI configuration |
# +-------------------+

<IfModule alias_module>
    # Sets up the location of your cgi-bin directory. More often
      than not you
    # will not use this. However, it can be useful to have this set
      up just in
    # case.
    ScriptAlias /cgi-bin/ "/usr/local/var/www/cgi-bin/"
</IfModule>

<Directory "/usr/local/var/www/cgi-bin">
    AllowOverride None
    Options None
    Require all granted
</Directory>

# +----------------------------+
```

158

```
# | Content-type configuration |
# +----------------------------+

<IfModule headers_module>
    #
    # Avoid passing HTTP_PROXY environment to CGI's on this or any proxied
    # backend servers which have lingering "httpoxy" defects.
    # 'Proxy' request header is undefined by the IETF, not listed by IANA
    #
    RequestHeader unset Proxy early
</IfModule>

<IfModule mime_module>
    #
    # TypesConfig points to the file containing the list of mappings from
    # filename extension to MIME-type.
    #
    TypesConfig /usr/local/etc/httpd/mime.types

    # Set up default types for compressed files. This will tell Apache to
    # send these to the user as downloads instead of trying to
      display them to
    # the browser.
    AddType application/x-compress .Z
    AddType application/x-gzip .gz .tgz
</IfModule>

# Configure mod_proxy_html to understand HTML4/XHTML1
<IfModule proxy_html_module>
Include /usr/local/etc/httpd/extra/proxy-html.conf
</IfModule>

# Basic HTTPS support, required even if we haven't set up a secure
site yet.
<IfModule ssl_module>
SSLRandomSeed startup builtin
SSLRandomSeed connect builtin
</IfModule>
```

159

Once you've updated your `httpd.conf` file, test the configuration, then restart Apache. You should be able to access your site at `http://localhost/`.

Basic HTTPS Configuration

A basic Apache setup is perfect for a local development environment. As soon as you make this environment open to the Internet, however, you need to secure it with HTTPS. Chapter 5 goes into this in more depth.

For the most part, the setup is identical to the basic Apache configuration. I've outlined next the additions you'll want to make in each configuration file.

httpd.conf

First, you need to configure Apache to load the SSL module. Open `httpd.conf` and navigate to the module configuration section (the section with all the LoadModule directives). Add or uncomment the following line.

```
LoadModule ssl_module lib/httpd/modules/mod_ssl.so
```

This loads the SSL module. However, it still needs to be configured, which is done in a separate file that Apache needs to include. It is done by adding the following line to the end of `httpd.conf`.

```
Include /usr/local/etc/httpd/extra/httpd-ssl.conf
```

extra/httpd-ssl.conf

After the SSL module has been loaded, Apache needs some additional configuration for SSL to work well. It's recommended to keep this configuration file separate for easier editing. You also use this file for setting up the default host running on the secure port. If you are running multiple virtual hosts, they each have their own configuration file.

```
Listen 443

# Configure what cipher suite Apache will allow the client to use.
For better
# security, this shold be kpet at HIGH
SSLCipherSuite HIGH:!aNULL
```

```
# Configure the SSL Protocol we want to use. We'll stick with just
SSLv3 for
# better security.
SSLProtocol all -SSLv3

# Configure how the passphrase for the SSL certificate is gathered.
We'll stick
# with the built in process.
SSLPassPhraseDialog  builtin

# Configures how the SSL session is cached.
SSLSessionCache          shmcb:${APACHE_RUN_DIR}/ssl_scache(512000)
SSLSessionCacheTimeout  300

# +-------------------+
# | VirtualHost Setup |
# +-------------------+

<VirtualHost *:443>

    # Turn on SSL for this setup
    SSLEngine on

    # Host setup
    DocumentRoot "/var/www/sites/local.apachebook.com"
    ServerName local.apachebook.com
    ServerAdmin you@example.com

    # Other directives here
    ErrorLog ${APACHE_LOG_DIR}/local.apachebook.com-error.log
    CustomLog ${APACHE_LOG_DIR}/local.apachebook.com-access.log combined

    # SSL Configuration
    SSLCertificateFile /etc/letsencrypt/live/local.apachebook.com-0001/
    fullchain.pem
    SSLCertificateKeyFile /etc/letsencrypt/live/local.apachebook.com-0001/
    privkey.pem

</VirtualHost>
```

Adding Rewrite Rules to Provide Human-Readable URLs

Let's say you're writing a content management system, and you want to have nice, human-readable URLs for pages on the site instead of something like http:// localhost/index.php?route=contact-us.

Building on the preceding basic Apache configuration, let's use the AllowOverrides setting and create an additional file, .htaccess. The .htaccess file is placed in your site project directory and provides custom Apache directive overrides without the need to restart Apache.

This overriding becomes especially useful in virtual host situations, where you might want Apache configured differently, depending on the virtual host being accessed. It's also a commonly used technique for content management systems to provide "clean" URLs.

Here's an example of the content you might put into the .htaccess file, assuming that you're using the route parameter to indicate a specific page on the site. I've added comments to explain what each line is doing.

.htaccess

```
<IfModule mod_rewrite.c>
    # Turns the Rewrite module on in Apache. It's off by default
    # for performance reasons.
    RewriteEngine On

    # Apache will always treat a training slash as a folder request
    # and will return a 404, even if URL rewriting is available.
    # This section checks to see if a file or directory exists first,
    # and then removes the slash if one doesn't exist.
    RewriteCond %{REQUEST_FILENAME} !-d
    RewriteCond %{REQUEST_URI} (.+)/$
    RewriteRule ^ %1 [L,R=301]

    # Here's the important part of the rewrite. Apache will take everything
    # after the domain name and pass it along to index.php through
      the route
```

```
# parameter. For example, if the browser requests http://localhost/
  contact,
# Apache will quietly rewrite the URL as http://localhost/index.
  php?route=contact
#
# Before it does any of this, however, it will check to see if
  a file or
# directory already exists with the requested name. This is critical
  for assets
# like CSS, javascript, or image files used as part of the
  site's output.
RewriteCond %{REQUEST_FILENAME} !-d
RewriteCond %{REQUEST_FILENAME} !-f
RewriteRule ^ /index.php?route= [L]
```

```
</IfModule>
```

Save the changes to the .htaccess file and try it out! `http://localhost/contact` should be silently redirected to `http://localhost/index.php?route=contact`.

Setting up Multiple Hosts (One PHP and One Node.js)

Apache is really powerful in its ability to run multiple websites off of one server instance. I talk about this in more depth in Chapter 3.

Let's say you wanted to set up three virtual hosts on your computer to provide development environments for a sandbox (`http://localhost`), your portfolio site in PHP (`http://portfolio.local`), and a Node.js project (`http://nodejs.local`).

httpd.conf

Grab a copy of the basic `httpd.conf` from the first section of this chapter, and add the following lines to the end.

macOS and Windows

```
# Import the virtual host configuration files.
IncludeOptional /usr/local/etc/httpd/extra/httpd-portfolio.local.conf
IncludeOptional /usr/local/etc/httpd/extra/httpd-nodejs.local.conf
```

Linux

```
# Import the virtual host configuration files.
IncludeOptional /etc/apache/sites-enabled/*
```

Let's use these two files to separate the configuration for each virtual host. On macOS or Windows, you want to put these files in the extra directory. On Linux, these need to be added to the sites-enabled directory.

portfolio.local.conf

This follows the same format used in Chapter 3. Refer to that chapter for information on what each of these directives does.

```
# Define the virtual host settings for the local domain
<VirtualHost *:80>
    ServerAdmin hello@getshipton.com
    DocumentRoot "/Users/darren/code/portfolio"
    ServerName portfolio.local
    ErrorLog "/usr/local/var/log/httpd/portfolio.local-error_log"
    CustomLog "/usr/local/var/log/httpd/portfolio.local-access_log" common
</VirtualHost>

<Directory "/Users/darren/code/portfolio">
    AllowOverride All
    DirectoryIndex index.php index.html
    Options FollowSymLinks Multiviews
    MultiviewsMatch any
    Require all granted
</Directory>
```

Save the file, and let's move on to the next virtual host.

nodejs.local.conf

As discussed in Chapter 4, Apache can proxy requests to a Node application. This is useful for providing a simpler URL that's constantly available. Let's use the same configuration created in that chapter. Refer to it for more information about each directive.

```
<VirtualHost *:80>
    DocumentRoot "/Users/darren/code/nodejs"
    ServerName nodeapp.local

    # Set up Logging
    ErrorLog "/usr/local/var/log/httpd/nodejs.local-error_log"
    CustomLog "/usr/local/var/log/httpd/nodejs.local-access_log" common

    <IfModule mod_proxy.c>
        ProxyPass / http://nodejs.local:3000
        ProxyPassReverse / http://nodejs.local:3000/

        <Proxy *>
            Order allow,deny
            Allow from all
        </Proxy>
    </IfModule>
</VirtualHost>
```

Once you've updated your httpd.conf, test the configuration, then restart Apache. You should be able to access your sites at http://localhost/, http://portfolio. local/, and http://nodejs.local/. Don't forget that you have to edit your host file and start your Node.js application before doing this, however!

Protected Directory

If you set up your dev environments using a publicly accessible subdomain, you want to add some protection. There are a couple of reasons for this.

- You don't want search engines to index the content on your dev site, which would harm the rankings of your production site.

- You don't want any random person to be able to access the developer site, which might have issues or be vulnerable to attacks.

The best way to prevent this is to protect the development subdomain behind a password. This is covered in the "Using .htaccess Files" section in Chapter 2. Of course, that gets annoying *very* quickly when you're trying to build a site and need to access it frequently on multiple devices.

The following configuration gives you the best of both worlds. The development subdomain is accessible to all devices on your local network without a password. You can access it from your laptop, desktop, or tablet and never be bothered by an authentication prompt. People outside your local network—let's say a colleague or a client needing to do a review—are prompted for a password before being able to access the site. And if they don't have that password, they'll get an HTTP error.

Let's assume that addresses in your network follow the 192.168.x.x address format. That is, the IP address on the network for your laptop might be something like 192.168.0.131, whereas your iPad's IP address might be 192.168.0.132. You want to allow any device on your local network to access the website without anything getting in the way.

This configuration uses three core directives.

- `Allow`

- `Require` (and its associated directives: AuthType, AuthName, and AuthUserFile)

- `Satisfy`

The `Allow` directive specifies a hostname, IP address or range, or IP addresses in a whitelist for access.

The `Require` directive is used in tandem with authentication. This directive says that Apache needs a user to be valid before they can access the website.

When set to "any", the `Satisfy` directive sets an either/or scenario in Apache. If the user requesting the page is outside the 192.168.0.x IP address range, a login prompt is presented. Otherwise, an error page informs the user that they must authenticate on the Apache server.

httpd.conf

Grab a copy of the basic httpd.conf from the first section of this chapter, and add the following lines to the end.

macOS and Windows

```
# Import the virtual host configuration files.
IncludeOptional /usr/local/etc/httpd/extra/dev.mydomain.com.conf
```

Linux

```
# Import the virtual host configuration files.
IncludeOptional /etc/apache/sites-enabled/*
```

Let's use this file to separate the configuration for this virtual host. On macOS or Windows, you want to put this file in the extra directory. On Linux, this needs to be added to the sites-enabled directory.

dev.mydomain.com.conf

```
# Define the virtual host settings for the local domain
<VirtualHost *:80>
    ServerAdmin hello@getshipton.com
    DocumentRoot "/Users/darren/code/dev.mydomain.com"
    ServerName portfolio.local
    ErrorLog "/usr/local/var/log/httpd/dev.mydomain.com-error_log"
    CustomLog "/usr/local/var/log/httpd/dev.mydomain.com-access_log" common
</VirtualHost>

<Directory "/Users/darren/code/dev.mydomain.com" >
  Options Indexes Includes FollowSymLinks MultiViews ExecCGI
  AllowOverride All
  # Set up authentication
  AuthName "Developer Access Only"
  AuthType Basic
  AuthUserFile /Users/darren/code/dev.mydomain.com/.htpasswd
  Require valid-user
```

```
# Tells Apache what order to read the access rules
Order Allow, Deny

# Allow from any IP address that starts with 192.168
Allow from 192.168.0

# Deny from anyone else.
Deny from all

# If any of the above criteria are met, let 'em in.
Satisfy any

# If not, show them an error page
ErrorDocument 401 /Users/darren/code/dev.mydomain.com/blocked.php
</Directory>
```

Epilogue

Welcome to the end of the book.

You've gone through quite the journey! You started by gently breaking into the world of configuring Apache by editing the `httpd.conf` file, opening your eyes to the inner workings of Apache. You even worked through some pretty complicated stuff, such as configuring virtual hosts and proxying.

Throughout this book, I've focused on using Apache for development environments on your computer. But here's a secret I can now reveal: it's no different configuring it on a remote production server. After reading this book and putting it into practice, you can now install, configure, and maintain an Apache server for your organization without fear, and go on to do great things.

Keep Learning

But your journey isn't over yet. Like all skills, you must keep learning. Apache is as complicated and full-featured as Figma or Illustrator, and while you have a good base of knowledge to work on, there's still a *lot* to learn.

Apache documentation is a great place to start. Now that you have enough base knowledge to find your way around, you'll better understand the more arcane configuration directives and be able to tune your Apache server to your needs.

Several other resources are available to you online, including the Apache website and community websites such as `https://community.apache.org`. Also, don't hesitate to visit Apache newsgroups or seek out an Apache user group in your area.

Maybe even talk to your local IT nerd from time to time.

You're now a digital deity—nothing can stop you!

© Darren James Harkness 2022
D. J. Harkness, *Apache Essentials*, https://doi.org/10.1007/978-1-4842-8324-0

APPENDIX

HTTP Status Codes

HTTP Status Codes

The following tables are reproduced from Wikipedia's "List of HTTP status codes" article (`https://en.wikipedia.org/wiki/List_of_HTTP_status_codes`). Don't be intimidated by the number of potential status codes. Generally, you will only encounter a few of these.

1xx Informational Response

An informational response indicates that the request was received and understood. It is issued on a provisional basis while request processing continues. It alerts the client to wait for a final response. The message consists only of the status line and optional header fields and is terminated by an empty line. As the HTTP/1.0 standard did not define any 1xx status codes, servers must not send a 1xx response to an HTTP/1.0 compliant client except under experimental conditions.

© Darren James Harkness 2022
D. J. Harkness, *Apache Essentials*, https://doi.org/10.1007/978-1-4842-8324-0

Table A-1. *100-Level Error Codes*

HTTP Code	Description
100 Continue	The server has received the request headers, and the client should proceed to send the request body (in the case of a request for which a body needs to be sent; for example, a POST request). Sending a large request body to a server after a request has been rejected for inappropriate headers would be inefficient. To have a server check the request's headers, a client must send Expect: 100-continue as a header in its initial request and receive a 100 Continue status code in response before sending the body. If the client receives an error code such as 403 (Forbidden) or 405 (Method Not Allowed), it should not send the request's body. The response 417 Expectation Failed indicates that the request should be repeated without the Expect header as the server does not support expectations (this is the case, for example, of HTTP/1.0 servers).
101 Switching Protocols	The requester has asked the server to switch protocols, and the server has agreed to do so.
102 Processing (WebDAV; RFC 2518)	A WebDAV request may contain many sub-requests involving file operations, requiring a long time to complete the request. This code indicates that the server has received and is processing the request, but no response is available. This prevents the client from timing out and assuming the request was lost.
103 Early Hints (RFC 8297)	This returns some response headers before the final HTTP message.

2xx Success

This class of status codes indicates the action requested by the client was received, understood, and accepted.

Table A-2. *200-Level Error Codes*

HTTP Code	Description
200 OK	Standard response for successful HTTP requests. The actual response depends on the request method used. In a GET request, the response contains an entity corresponding to the requested resource. In a POST request, the response contains an entity describing or containing the result of the action.
201 Created	The request has been fulfilled, resulting in the creation of a new resource.
202 Accepted	The request has been accepted for processing, but the processing has not been completed. The request might or might not be eventually acted upon and may be disallowed when processing occurs.
203 Non-Authoritative Information (since HTTP/1.1)	The server is a transforming proxy (e.g., a Web accelerator) that received a 200 OK from its origin but is returning a modified version of the origin's response.
204 No Content	The server successfully processed the request and is not returning any content.
205 Reset Content	The server successfully processed the request, asks that the requester reset its document view, and is not returning any content.
206 Partial Content (RFC 7233)	The server is delivering only part of the resource (byte serving) due to a range header sent by the client. HTTP clients use the range header to enable resuming of interrupted downloads or split a download into multiple simultaneous streams.
207 Multi-Status (WebDAV; RFC 4918)	The message body that follows is an XML message and can contain many separate response codes, depending on how many sub-requests were made.
208 Already Reported (WebDAV; RFC 5842)	The members of a DAV binding have already been enumerated in a preceding part of the (multi-status) response and are not being included again.
226 IM Used (RFC 3229)	The server has fulfilled a request for the resource, and the response represents the result of one or more instance manipulations applied to the current instance.

3xx Redirection

This class of status code indicates the client must take additional action to complete the request. Many of these status codes are used in URL redirection.

A user agent may carry out the additional action with no user interaction only if the method used in the second request is GET or HEAD. A user agent may automatically redirect a request. A user agent should detect and intervene to prevent cyclical redirects.

Table A-3. *300-Level Error Codes*

HTTP Code	Description
300 Multiple Choices	Indicates multiple options for the resource from which the client may choose (via agent-driven content negotiation). For example, this code could present multiple video format options, list files with different filename extensions, or suggest word-sense disambiguation.
301 Moved Permanently	This and all future requests should be directed to the given URI.
302 Found (previously Moved Temporarily)	Tells the client to look at (browse to) another URL. The HTTP/1.0 specification (RFC 1945) required the client to perform a temporary redirect with the same method (the original describing phrase was Moved Temporarily), but popular browsers implemented 302 redirects by changing the method to GET. Therefore, HTTP/1.1 added status codes 303 and 307 to distinguish between the two behaviors.
303 See Other (since HTTP/1.1)	The response to the request can be found under another URI using the GET method. When received in response to a POST (or PUT/DELETE), the client should presume that the server has received the data and issue a new GET request to the URI.
304 Not Modified (RFC 7232)	The resource has not been modified since the version specified by the request headers If-Modified-Since or If-None-Match. In such a case, there is no need to retransmit the resource since the client still has a previously-downloaded copy.

(continued)

Table A-3. (*continued*)

HTTP Code	Description
305 Use Proxy (since HTTP/1.1)	The requested resource is available only through a proxy, the address provided in the response. For security reasons, many HTTP clients (such as Mozilla Firefox and Internet Explorer) do not obey this status code.
306 Switch Proxy	No longer used. Originally meant, "Subsequent requests should use the specified proxy."
307 Temporary Redirect (since HTTP/1.1)	In this case, the request should be repeated with another URI; however, future requests should still use the original URI. In contrast to how 302 was historically implemented, the request method cannot be changed when reissuing the original request. For example, a POST request should be repeated using another POST request.
308 Permanent Redirect (RFC 7538)	This and all future requests should be directed to the given URI. 308 parallels the behavior of 301 but does not allow the HTTP method to change. So, for example, submitting a form to a permanently redirected resource may continue smoothly.

4xx Client Errors

This class of status code is intended for situations in which the error seems to have been caused by the client. Except when responding to a HEAD request, the server should include an entity containing an explanation of the error situation and whether it is a temporary or permanent condition. These status codes apply to any request method. User agents should display any included entity to the user.

Table A-4. *400-Level Error Codes*

HTTP Code	Description
400 Bad Request	The server cannot or will not process the request due to an apparent client error (e.g., malformed request syntax, size too large, invalid request message framing, or deceptive request routing).
401 Unauthorized (RFC 7235)	Similar to 403 Forbidden, but specifically for use when authentication is required and has failed or has not yet been provided. The response must include a WWW-Authenticate header field containing a challenge applicable to the requested resource. See Basic access authentication and Digest access authentication. 401 semantically means "unauthorized," the user does not have valid authentication credentials for the target resource. Note: Some sites incorrectly issue HTTP 401 when an IP address is banned from the website (usually the website domain), and that specific address is refused permission to access a website.
402 Payment Required	Reserved for future use. The original intention was that this code might be used as part of some form of digital cash or micropayment scheme, as proposed, for example, by GNU Taler, but that has not yet happened, and this code is not widely used. Google Developers API uses this status if a particular developer has exceeded the daily limit on requests. Sipgate uses this code if an account does not have sufficient funds to start a call. Shopify uses this code when the store has not paid its fees and is temporarily disabled. Stripe uses this code for failed payments where parameters were correct, for example, blocked fraudulent payments.

(continued)

Table A-4. (*continued*)

HTTP Code	Description
403 Forbidden	The request contained valid data and was understood by the server, but the server is refusing action. This may be due to the user not having the necessary permissions for a resource or needing an account of some sort, or attempting a prohibited action (e.g., creating a duplicate record where only one is allowed). This code is also typically used if the request provided authentication by answering the WWW-Authenticate header field challenge, but the server did not accept that authentication. The request should not be repeated.
404 Not Found	The requested resource could not be found but may be available in the future. Subsequent requests by the client are permissible.
405 Method Not Allowed	A request method is not supported for the requested resource; for example, a GET request on a form that requires data to be presented via POST or a PUT request on a read-only resource.
406 Not Acceptable	The requested resource can generate only content not acceptable according to the Accept headers sent in the request. See Content negotiation.
407 Proxy Authentication Required (RFC 7235)	The client must first authenticate itself with the proxy.
408 Request Timeout	The server timed out, waiting for the request. According to HTTP specifications: "The client did not produce a request within the time that the server was prepared to wait. The client may repeat the request without modifications at any later time."

(*continued*)

Table A-4. (*continued*)

HTTP Code	Description
409 Conflict	Indicates that the request could not be processed because of conflict in the current state of the resource, such as an edit conflict between multiple simultaneous updates.
410 Gone	Indicates that the resource requested is no longer available. This should be used when a resource has been intentionally removed, and the resource should be purged. Upon receiving a 410 status code, the client should not request the resource in the future. Clients such as search engines should remove the resource from their indices. Most use cases do not require clients and search engines to purge the resource, and a 404 Not Found may be used instead.
411 Length Required	The request did not specify the length of its content, which is required by the requested resource.
412 Precondition Failed (RFC 7232)	The server does not meet one of the preconditions that the requester put on the request header fields.
413 Payload Too Large (RFC 7231)	The request is larger than the server is willing or able to process. Previously called Request Entity Too Large.
414 URI Too Long (RFC 7231)	The URI provided was too long for the server to process. Often the result of too much data is encoded as a query string of a GET request, in which case it should be converted to a POST request. Previously called Request-URI Too Long.
415 Unsupported Media Type (RFC 7231)	The request entity has a media type that the server or resource does not support. For example, the client uploads an image as image/svg+xml, but the server requires that images use a different format.
416 Range Not Satisfiable (RFC 7233)	The client has asked for a portion of the file (byte serving), but the server cannot supply that portion. For example, if the client asked for a part of the file that lies beyond the end of the file. Previously called Requested Range Not Satisfiable.

(*continued*)

Table A-4. (*continued*)

HTTP Code	Description
417 Expectation Failed	The server cannot meet the requirements of the Expect request-header field.
418 I'm a teapot (RFC 2324, RFC 7168)	This code was defined in 1998 as one of the traditional IETF April Fools' jokes in RFC 2324, HyperText Coffee Pot Control Protocol, and is not expected to be implemented by actual HTTP servers. The RFC specifies this code should be returned by teapots requested to brew coffee. This HTTP status is used as an Easter egg on some websites, such as the Google "I'm a teapot" Easter egg.
421 Misdirected Request (RFC 7540)	The request was directed at a server unable to produce a response (for example, because of connection reuse).
422 Unprocessable Entity (WebDAV; RFC 4918)	The request was well-formed but was unable to be followed due to semantic errors.
423 Locked (WebDAV; RFC 4918)	The resource that is being accessed is locked.
424 Failed Dependency (WebDAV; RFC 4918)	The request failed because it depended on another request, and that request failed (e.g., a PROPPATCH).
425 Too Early (RFC 8470)	This indicates that the server is unwilling to risk processing a request that might be replayed.
426 Upgrade Required	The client should switch to a different protocol, such as TLS/1.3, given in the Upgrade header field.
428 Precondition Required (RFC 6585)	The origin server requires the request to be conditional. Intended to prevent the 'lost update' problem, where a client GETs a resource's state, modifies it, and PUTs it back to the server when a third party has modified the state on the server, leading to a conflict.
429 Too Many Requests (RFC 6585)	The user has sent too many requests in a given amount of time. Intended for use with rate-limiting schemes.

(*continued*)

Table A-4. (*continued*)

HTTP Code	Description
431 Request Header Fields Too Large (RFC 6585)	The server is unwilling to process the request because either an individual header field or all the header fields collectively are too large.
451 Unavailable For Legal Reasons (RFC 7725)	A server operator has received a legal demand to deny access to a resource or to a set of resources that includes the requested resource. Code 451 was chosen as a reference to the novel Fahrenheit 451 (see the Acknowledgements in the RFC).

5xx Server Errors

The server failed to fulfill a request.

Response status codes beginning with the digit 5 indicate cases in which the server is aware that it has encountered an error or is otherwise incapable of performing the request. Except when responding to a HEAD request, the server should include an entity containing an explanation of the error situation and indicate whether it is a temporary or permanent condition. Likewise, user agents should display any included entity to the user. These response codes apply to any request method.

Table A-5. *500-Level Error Codes*

HTTP Code	Description
500 Internal Server Error	A generic error message is given when an unexpected condition is encountered, and no more specific message is suitable.
501 Not Implemented	The server either does not recognize the request method or cannot fulfill the request. Usually, this implies future availability (e.g., a new feature of a web-service API).
502 Bad Gateway	The server acted as a gateway or proxy and received an invalid response from the upstream server.
503 Service Unavailable	The server cannot handle the request (because it is overloaded or down for maintenance). Generally, this is a temporary state.
504 Gateway Timeout	The server acted as a gateway or proxy and did not receive a timely response from the upstream server.
505 HTTP Version Not Supported	The server does not support the HTTP protocol version used in the request.
506 Variant Also Negotiates (RFC 2295)	Transparent content negotiation for the request results in a circular reference.
507 Insufficient Storage (WebDAV; RFC 4918)	The server is unable to store the representation needed to complete the request.
508 Loop Detected (WebDAV; RFC 5842)	The server detected an infinite loop while processing the request (sent instead of 208 Already Reported).
510 Not Extended (RFC 2774)	Further extensions to the request are required for the server to fulfill it.
511 Network Authentication Required (RFC 6585)	The client needs to authenticate to gain network access. Intended for use by intercepting proxies to control access to the network (e.g., "captive portals" to require agreement to terms of service before granting full Internet access via a Wi-Fi hotspot).

Index

© Darren James Harkness 2022
D. J. Harkness, *Apache Essentials*, https://doi.org/10.1007/978-1-4842-8324-0

Printed in the United States
by Baker & Taylor Publisher Services